Isaiah 60:1-3
Thanks
Wynette-

Look What Jesus Did!

A Divine Outlook of the Person of Jesus Christ

W. A. Tyrrell

Look What Jesus Did!
A Divine Outlook of the Person of Jesus Christ

Kingdom Publishing, LLC
1350 Blair Drive
Odenton, MD 21113

Printed in the U.S.A.

All scripture quotations are from the King James Version of the Bible. Thomas Nelson Publishers, Nashville: Thomas Nelson, Inc. 1972.

Picture sketch of Jesus drawn by Mykelle Lockley

Library of Congress Control Number: 2018946262

ISBN 978-1-947741-13-3

Dedication

With a humble heart of gratitude, I dedicate this book to the Father God - Elohim, the Judge and Creator of all; to my Lord and Savior Jesus Christ and the Bishop and the Shepherd of my soul, and to the Holy Ghost my Comforter and Guide. I must admit, "If I should write about your amazing Love, I would run out of paper."

I dedicate this book also, to my honey and best friend, for your support, and encouragement to believe in God, and myself during this journey. From a technical prospective as you taught me to appreciate today, that all airplanes do encounter turbulence in flight. My story account could be related with your terminology. I would not be alive to this day, without you and my God-fearing sons' faithfulness. Thank you all, for praying with me throughout these years.

Acknowledgments

I wish to thank, Bishop Kibby, with a grateful heart. I have been privileged to know and respect this great man of God, such a prototype of the love of God. Thanks for your intercession prayers and dedication to enforce the blessings of God upon my life. I do appreciate all your support of my family and my situations during this journey. Thank you also, for the powerful men of God, you had included in our presence. Indeed Sir: "LOOK WHAT THE LORD HAS DONE!"

Table of Contents

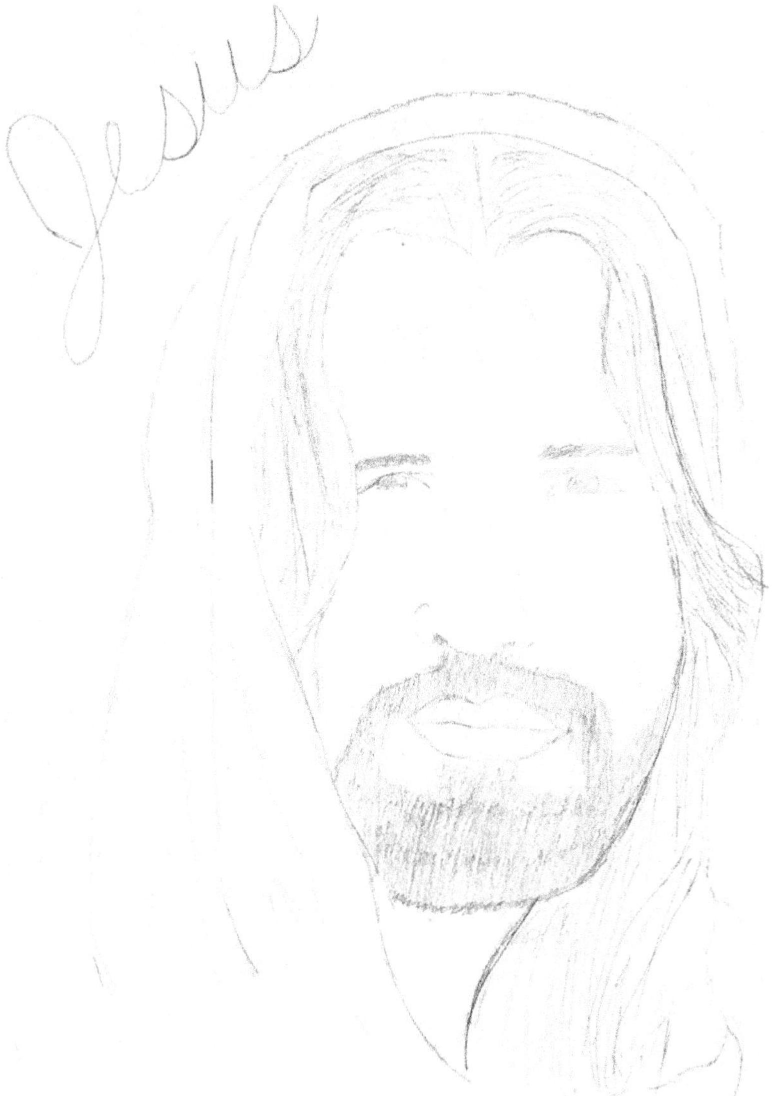
Jesus

Introduction

Look What Jesus Did!

I thank the Lord Jesus and the Holy Ghost for strengthening me to accomplish this task and reiterate to you this fact. With a humble heart, it is a privilege to declare to you He is Alive. I have learnt that Jesus has an awesome personality. Throughout these stories my intention is to encourage you to have encounters and share your revelations of Jesus Christ. I wanted you to understand I found safety in knowing it is a great place to walk with the Lord.

Throughout this book there are practical outlooks of the divine dimensions of the Lord Jesus Christ. As an ordinary believer, these experiences and revelations would truly promote an intimate lifestyle of the Love of Jesus. This book will cause you to take to another level the challenge of a friendship of the Lord Jesus. It was also designed to have you take a direct step into a Love walk with Jesus Christ.

Regardless of your religious faith and imperfections the Lord Jesus Christ wants to have pleasure in appearing and revealing himself to you. As you develop a desire to experience him, the personal encounter with you will eventually happen. Through these meetings you will learn to appreciate the way the Lord uses dreams and visions to also make His presence known.

'Jesus is Real! and He is Alive! He Loves You and wants to be your friend!'

Maybe you are asking how you can explore His love and friendship. It is simple; as you allow the Holy Spirit to take precedence in your life along with your prayer and reading of the Word of God, the Holy Spirit will lead you as His presence will be manifested through the gifts. In time, you will develop a stronger desire as His spirit guides you into an intimate fellowship with the Lord Jesus Christ. The Bible declares, 'Ask and it shall be given you, seek, and you shall find; knock, and it shall be opened unto you.' - Matthew 11:9-19

Jesus loves you even in your imperfect state, but He is a gentleman and He will not intervene in your life unless you let Him. His love, His mercy and His compassion are the testimony of my life. The beautiful thing about Jesus is that you will get to represent Him as a kingdom ambassador. As you let Him into your life He will give you a desire to encourage others to seek after His Love.

There are many people who were captivated by Jesus's appearances in their lives and situations. I found out through a research, that they also had a desire to share, but were scared to tell because of persecution from others. I began to develop and grow spiritually as the encounters progressed and I began to trust Jesus during this process. The Lord encouraged me to write these encounters as an encouragement to say to you, they are normal as in the bible.

The burden to share my awesome experiences became more evident as time went on. I realized that the Lord has ways to change your mindset supernaturally in fulfilling his purpose. In a dreams Jesus instructed me to name this Book, 'LOOK WHAT JESUS DID!' and he went on as details of the type of cover was later revealed.

Chapter One

Our Precious Inheritance

Blessed is the Man whom thou choose, and causes to approach unto thee, that he may dwell in thy courts: we shall be satisfied with the goodness of thy house even of the Holy Temple.

Psalm 65:4

Could you imagine, God with his credentials fitted in your imaginary box?

Unfortunately, most believers are guilty of placing God into a box. Therefore, as events take place outside those parameters of their understanding, they will consistently reject the supernatural occurrences, because their imaginations are limited.

During this journey of my spiritual walk with the Lord, I had heard and experienced the Father, the Son and the Holy Ghost at different times - 1 John 5:7. It became understandable that God loved to use dreams and visions as a tool to promote his agenda in our lives. Eventually, I began to recognize and learn the true revelation of the three Personalities of God with whom we have encounter. Many spiritual truths began to be downloaded in my spirit and the reference to each of these events you will read later in the book.

Throughout the bible, God always spoke to mankind as He came down from the heavens, and even today, He is doing so. The Lord spoke to His people in dreams and visions and at other times He appeared to them. However, modern Christianity has tried to minimize the teachings about God's chastening, dreams and visions. As a result of the limited exposure to intimacy with the Lord and the Holy Spirit in the church, it has interfered with the individual believer's experience today.

Church has become more about the grace factor, and the prophetic dream experiences on a personal level with the person of Jesus Christ are deemed as evil and absent. In most religious institutions, there is a scarcity of spiritual mature people who are helpful to explain the complexity of God's gifts to the believer. The Lord Jesus is the Bishop and Shepherd of your souls (1 Peter 2:25). I became aware that He can supernaturally reveal himself to you through the Word of God and the Holy Spirit.

The path of righteousness that King David referred to in Psalms 23, meant that your dream encounters and struggles are part of your experiences in life. Have you stopped to consider that there is some measure of the Holy Spirit encounter on a daily basis?

His love for you had included His presence in His plans. In contrast to the breath of air you breathe daily to sustain your life, God wanted mankind to be infused with a fresh tangible relationship of His presence. The bible declared, the Lord God formed man from the dust of the ground, and breathed into his nostrils the breath of life; and man became a living soul (Genesis 2:7).

The Lord's plan and desire for His creation was for you to love and worship Him and do His work. He keeps looking for ones that would capture His heart. His intentions are to fellowship with you throughout your life and ministry. These special gifts are used through the blood of Jesus Christ to set at liberty those who the evil one tried to possess. His commission is for all believers to demonstrate God's love and authority in the power of the Holy Spirit for healing and deliverance. Jesus wants you to serve Him so that the devil will not have anything to gloat about.

The Lord God has no preference or limitations to whom He chooses to speak or share His visions and dreams with. This means that Jesus can have frequent visitation with whom He desires.

And it shall come to pass afterwards, that I will pour out my Spirit upon all flesh; And your sons and your daughters shall prophesy, your old men shall dream dreams, your men shall see visions.
Joel 2:28

God's supernatural gift of dreams, visions and revelations are your inheritance today. I pray that your spiritual eyes be enlightened, and you would not lose your focus on His promises.

Chapter Two

His Divine Presence

Surely the Lord God will do nothing, but he revealeth his secret unto his servants the prophets.

Amos 3:7

The story of Jesus Christ dying on the Cross is the first acknowledgement of His love. Through your obedience to the Word of God you have an inheritance of His presence, especially to those who walk upright with the Almighty God.

The Holy Ghost played a vital role as the Lord's mouth piece after Jesus Christ departed into heaven. He told them he would send the Holy Spirit to teach us all truth. Jesus said, the Comforter will reveal all things to you (John 14:26).

HIS DREAMS

The Lord is gracious and plenteous in mercy. The Lord could appear in the day or night-time. He also sends angels to appear to you and bring His messages.

His demeanor is very gentle, and because of this He could be easily ignored. He speaks through the Holy Spirit in many instances, and many people do not recognize His divine presence is as near as a simple prayers. Through His spirit He is constantly communing with you but the cares of the world often muffles His voice; simply because you are somewhat distracted while you are awake. As a loving God by nature, He patiently waits until the nighttime to come and commune in dreams. In other words, this is God's way of getting your undivided attention as you are in stillness of a deep sleep. At these times it seems less difficult for your minds to reject the supernatural working of His thoughts.

Jesus desires conversation with you as He loves to respond to your prayers. His divine presence is mostly imminent through dreams and visions as He downloads His secrets to you. It is a privilege to understand some ways that the Lord loves to bring sneak peeks of things to come in the future or warnings to prevent certain situations.

God could use dreams to rebuke your enemies on your behalf. The bible tells of the story of Jacob and his uncle Laban. In a dream the Lord spoke to Laban to release Jacob (Genesis 31:12).

Other dream experiences that the Lord God Almighty allowed in your life are sometimes buffeting dreams which can be disturbing. These dreams have a way of getting your attention as they usually produce more intense intercessory prayer. God also uses dreams as a dimension of His divine presence to urge us to pray and intercede for others. I found out that not everything that goes on in your life is from the evil one, but sometimes the Lord permits the evil to chasten the righteous. In the case of King Saul God used an evil spirit to chasten him because of sin, but David interceded for Saul in worship.

Have you considered how Jesus needs you to fulfill His purposes?

The Lord needs someone to speak on His behalf and do His works; this is why He uses His divine presence to commune with you. The Bible declared that the Word of God is wisdom and the foundation of the supernatural (Ephesians 1:17-19).

For God speaketh once, yea twice, yet man perceiveth it not. In a dream, in a vision of the night, when in deep sleep falleth upon men, in slumberings upon the bed; Then he openeth the ears of men, and sealeth their instructions.

Job 33:14-16

HIS REVELATIONS

The bible declared, God is an all-knowing God and the Revealer of all things. He loves to reveal things to you, even today.

The Bible declared, the Wise men being warned in a dream, that they should not return to Herod, they departed into their own country another way (Matthew 2:12).

At the same hour Joseph as the wise men departed, behold in a dream as the angel of the Lord appeared and said, 'Arise, and take the young child and his mother, and flee to Egypt' (Matthew 2:13).

In the days of long ago as God saw that the heart of man had become wicked, God talked with Noah and revealed his unhappiness towards the people and the type of destruction He had in mind. God also asked him to design a boat with special specifications in preparation for the flood.

The bible said, God revealed his intentions to flood the earth to Noah (Genesis 6:13).

The Word of God in many instances has revealed that the Lord uses His divine presence to reveal His plans. His dreams and revelations could be given in different ways. The stories told of revelations of

Daniel and Joseph were a few examples. It was shown that the Lord had different responses for each of their prayers. In one case there was an instantaneous revealing and in the other it took time. The lesson learned was that Patience is key, as we pray and seek God for answers.

The Lord declared, 'For my thoughts are not your thoughts, neither are your ways my ways.' (Isaiah 55:8).

The Bible declared that, King Nebuchadnezzar had dreamt and was disturbed about not remembering his dreams. As Daniel appeared before the king he offered to help but he requested that the king give him time. The scriptures declared that Daniel inquired of the God of Heaven, and while asleep the Lord came to him and revealed the dream.

Then, was the secret revealed unto Daniel in a night vision. Then Daniel blessed the God of Heaven.
Daniel 2: 19

The Pharaoh's dreams were told to Joseph, and Joseph inquired of the Lord, and immediately he received the interpretation of the dreams the bible declared (Genesis 41:15-37).

These were great example of how you should address complex situations, especially when they are dreams that we cannot understand. The story of King Solomon is a typical example. The Bible said that God appeared to Solomon many times in the night and spoke in dreams. The Lord spoke with him about the blessings and wisdom He would grant to him. In another dream the Lord came to warn Solomon of the consequences of his sin should he turn away in disobedience.

The Lord appeared by night, and said unto him, I have heard thy prayer, and have chosen this place to myself for a house of sacrifice.
2 Chronicles 7:12

JESUS THE MYSTERY

An Appetizer for your thoughts! Amongst the incredible stories in Genesis, this revelation was a divine intervention of the Lord. In Genesis 28, Jacob's encounter was supernatural as he was given the vision of what transpires when you pray. The occurrence of the constant communication between heaven and earth was revealed in his dream. The bible said that Jesus was standing at the top of the ladder, and the angels were employed as ministering spirits to serve all the wisdom and purposes of the Lord. The continuous ascending and descending was for service to us day and night.

The Bible goes on to say that Jacob wrestled with an angel. As Jacob inquired of his name, the angel did not reveal his name, but instead changed Jacob's name. The revelation of who the angel could have been I received by reading the word of God. I am convinced that the one Jacob wrestled with was the pre-incarnated Christ, even though he didn't say His name.

There was another mystery which has some relevance. The Bible declared that the angel who appeared to Samson's parents also did not say his name. In their persistence to know the angel's name, the bible declared that the angel said, 'It was secret,' and he did *wonderful* acts before them, when he went up toward heaven from off the altar (Judges 13: 17-19).

Could it be that the unnamed angel in the Scriptures was referred to the name "wonderful" in the scripture, Isaiah 9:6, 'For unto us a child is born, unto us a son is given: and the government shall be upon his shoulder: and his name shall be called *WONDERFUL*, Counsellor, The Almighty God, The Everlasting Father, The Prince of Peace.'

As you allow your hearts to be open to the Lord, He will fill you with wisdom and understanding.

Chapter Three

The Lord Revealed

One thing have I desired of the Lord, that will I seek after; that I may dwell in the house of the Lord all the days of my life, to behold the beauty of the Lord, and to inquire in his Temple.
Psalm 27:4

HIS ENCOUNTER

It was in the middle of July a few years ago, during an experience of a complicated pregnancy that resulted in the loss of my baby girl. I had fallen to sleep one evening and something supernatural happened to me. I was caught up into the heaven and I encountered Jesus face to face. I found myself by a riverside and Jesus stood at my right-side. He began to speak as He mentioned the place we were standing was by the river of 'Living' water. I could see that the water was transparent, crystal clear; however, I was not permitted to touch or cross over to the other side.

The heavenly atmosphere was very peaceful, and there was no sense of chaos present. I felt my heart say it was the place I should stay. I was contented to be there with Jesus. I began to look around the riverside; there it seemed like everything was alive, the flowers and the trees were alive, they seemed to all move in symphony and harmony in the presence of the Lord. I looked and there I saw two angels dressed in long white robes gazing in our direction as they stood a little way off.

After a few moments, Jesus took time to show me the outcome of my tragedy. My baby Tricia was there with him and I felt an overwhelming peace come over me as I trusted him. Eventually, He spoke and instructed me to return home, as he said, there was an assignment he needed me to finish. My heart felt sad as I had no desire to return, as I thought it was too evil over there. Jesus stood with his eyes penetrating my heart affectionately, as I pleaded and cried for him to let me stay. He knew my every thought, as I had not planned to leave without a fuss.

It seemed like Jesus was prepared as suddenly He turned his gaze in the direction of the angels. I saw them coming and there they stood next to me on both sides. Finally, Jesus crossed the river slowly with my loved one. I cried loudly as they faded way, then I felt them grip my arms and I was zapped swiftly into the earth. I was back in my bed.

I was distraught for a long time as the taste of Heaven still lingered in my mind. I could not bring myself to discuss my experience with anyone. I knew they wouldn't understand as I didn't grieve for my loss. I still kept pondering as the time went by, what was Jesus reason for my return anyway. It was revealed to me a few years ago that my return was for my family in crisis. As Jesus assured me He still wanted to be with me upon the earth.

To every mother who lost a baby, this story would reassure you that every lost child is in heaven with God the Father and Jesus.

THE TIME OF FELLOWSHIP

And in the morning, rising up a great while before day, he (Jesus) went out,
and departed into a solitary place, and there he prayed.

Mark 1:35

JESUS FAVORITE TIMES

It was early one morning at 3 a.m. and this encounter really blew my mind as Jesus appeared to me. He said, this was His favorite time for fellowship. He kept coming in my dreams constantly for a few days at this particular time and I found myself expecting His visitation. One morning the Lord prompted me to study the word of God to find what it had said concerning His communing with His Father.

Eventually, the Holy Ghost took over and I had no need for an alarm clock. I would just awake early in the morning to commune with Him. It became a time for worship and revelations. I heard one man explain it, as a time of His divine acceleration in your life.

The scriptures recorded that Jesus was an early morning person. It was during a time long before dawn, and at a place away from everyone and everything that Jesus communed with His Father. The Hebrew Sages said, it was on these occasions Jesus may have told His Father all the events of the day before and He received the task for the day ahead from His Father.

Then as Jesus came down, He was moved with compassion and healed all that were diseased and all those possessed by devils. As He spoke to His disciple Jesus told them, He only heard and did what his father told him to do.

And Jesus went forth, and saw a great multitude, and was moved with
compassion towards them, and he healed their sick. (Matthew 14:14)

HIS MOUNTAIN

Jesus's love for the mountain was in relevance to the word of God. There are many revelations in the bible pertaining to the Mountain experiences that God desired as a meeting place. Abraham declared, He was the God of the mountains.

The scene upon the Mountain was a foreshadow of Jesus Christ, as the Lord asked Abraham to sacrifice his only son Isaac. The bible said, Abraham trusted God and there he was provided a Ram in the picket. In another instance, God spoke to Moses and asked him to come up on the mountain to receive the Ten Commandments. Afterwards, He gave him details of the service of the Tabernacle, before the people of Israel crossed over to the promise Land. Eventually, God also told Aaron to come up to the mountain to strip him of his priestly duties because of the sin of the Golden Calf.

Chapter Four

His Character

HIS FRIENDSHIP

I call you not servants; for the servant knoweth not what his lord doeth: but I have called you friends; for all things that I have heard of my Father I have made know unto you.

John 15:15

The Lord is a tangible friend; I have no other explanation for my declaration. Jesus has a very loving and gentle demeanor. In a dream 'He appeared to me' and that encounter blew all my fears away. He really loves to have intimate friendships and conversations with you. Jesus has offered an everlasting friendship as your Lord and King like no other could.

A friendship with Jesus is very accessible. Usually you meet people along the journey of life and you hope for friendships that would grow and develop into loving relationships. Well this is the same way you can cultivate a relationship with Jesus that could grow and become as awesome as your natural friendships. As you begin to look through the lens of love as Jesus is love, it becomes easier as you gradually grow into an appreciation for His loving personality.

HIS LOVING KINDNESS

The love factor is simply what is most true about who you are. Jesus is the source and end of all real love and friendship. The bible declared, Jesus suffered and died on the cross to free us from all sins and condemnation. At the cross, the Lord Jesus Christ shed his blood as He paid the price for all our sins.

A simple key to a love relationship with Jesus is found in the book of Deuteronomy which declared, You shall Love the Lord, at all times.

This statement could clarify and entice you to a higher calling to see the scripture as a concept:

And thou shalt love the Lord thy God with all thine heart, and all thy soul, and with all thy might.
Deuteronomy 6:5

With all your heart: this implies that God has given you a new heart to love Him.

With all your soul: implies that you are enabled to truly feel the Lord, and that your heart is made tender and sensitized to Him.

With all your might: means all your 'substance'- that really makes you who you are in integrity and character according to the command of the Lord God.

There are no excuses! You don't have to let accusations and the mistakes you made hinder your relationship with the Lord. He included those weaknesses in His death and resurrection plan. It is necessary for true repentance unto redemption by the blood of Jesus on the cross.

The Word of God also proclaims; 'Trust in the Lord with all thine heart and lean not unto thine own understanding. In all thy ways acknowledge Him and He will direct your paths.' - Proverbs 3:5-6

A CHILDLIKE FAITH

In one dream, Jesus came and began to reveal to me the type of people who catch his attention. He showed me the childlike faith, how it touches the heart of the Father. I was positioned to observe a few children, and I could recognize how they love and trust Jesus with all their hearts. It was not complicated as I saw the confidence that they stood on as they knew Jesus would hear and answer their prayers.

I was shown a group of adults, and as I observed their reaction it was opposite to the children. They were very faithless and it was as if they found difficulty in trusting Jesus. He had sadness in His eyes as He heard their unbelief.

This was a great lesson I learned as I found the qualities of the children were so innocent, humble and contented. They were all in awe of the splendor of God's majesty. It was obvious they took God at his word in simplicity.

Except ye be converted, and become as a little child, ye shall not enter into the Kingdom of Heaven.
Matthew 18:3

Let me refresh your minds of the quality of an innocent child. It was noted that they exercise full assurance, as they came to their loving father and mother, to completely take care of them, to protect them, to provide for them, to correct them when they are wrong, to love and cherish them. God loves a childlike, meek and submissive heart of faith towards Him. The heart of God is moved by childlike love and faith.

HE LOVES YOU!

As the Father hath loved me, so have I loved you: Continue in my love.
John 15:9

It is extremely difficult to understand believers who threat others unkindly. They usually profess that Jesus lives inside of them but their reflection of his love is marred. This type of behavior is contradicting to the love of the Father. I find that the love of the Lord is infinite, and His love is detailed for every living creature upon the face of the earth.

The greatest commandment of God is to Love. Jesus declared if there was not love, then you are of your father the Devil, for God is Love!

The Bible declared, For God so loved the world that he gave his only begotten Son, that whosoever believeth in Him should not perish, but have everlasting life (John 3:16).

The Lord's Love for the tiny birds was portrayed in his commands to Moses as follow.

If a bird's nest chance to be before thee in the way in any tree, or on the ground, whether they be young ones, or eggs, and the dam sitting upon the young, or upon the eggs, thou shalt not take the Mother- dam with the young: But thou shall in any wise let the dam go, and take the young to thee; that it may be well with thee, and it will prolong thy days.
Deuteronomy 22:6-7

What manner of love the Father hath bestowed upon us, that we should be called, the Sons of God.
1 John 3:1

Chapter Five

His Glorious Visitation

HE IS ALIVE!

After a few years of challenges in my family life, I began to develop a great yearning to see the face of Jesus again. I started focusing many of my prayers with the desire and expectation of my request. I trusted Jesus would take care of the situations that were occurring. I constantly repented of my imperfections and believed in His forgiveness as I purposed in my heart to live a lifestyle of rejoicing and praise that continually accepted His joy.

In the Spring of 2015 my prayers were answered as Jesus revealed himself to me. I knew He had heard my pleas without a shadow of doubt and this appearance caused me to become a junkie for His presence, to put it mildly. Something supernatural happened and I could not get enough of Jesus, my King, my Lord and Saviour.

I guarantee He will respond to you, just keep asking Jesus for an encounter. His promise of love and friendship is in your obedience to the word of God. The picture frame of your future will become brightened with love and confidence and this will lead you to a new perceptive of dreams.

In the bible there was a great revelation and outlook of the Lord in His Majesty as His presence and personality were revealed by the prophet Ezekiel (Ezekiel 1:26-29).

Only the Holy Spirit can reveal and explain such revelations. The bible declared through visions, the Lord showed the prophet Daniel and John the Revelator, the future of the world to come. He also allowed the prophet Ezekiel to have a vision of the Heavenly throne.

Every believer needs the Lord to give them supernatural wisdom, and the gift of understanding for the scriptures. The mind naturally does not have the capacity to comprehend the secrets of future events. Can you really imagine, for instance, the promise to you, as a partaker of the New Jerusalem, or the wedding supper of the Lord?

John saw in a vision, a new heaven and a new earth. He saw a holy city, a New Jerusalem, coming down from God out of heaven prepared, as a bride adorned for her groom (Revelation 21:1-4).

"That which we have seen and heard declare we unto to you, that ye also may fellowship with us: and truly our fellowship is with the Father and with the Son Jesus Christ."
1 John 1:3

MY AWESOME EXPERIENCE

It was during a period of prayer and fasting that Jesus appeared. At evening, before I go to sleep I often worship with these words 'Lord I want to see your face.' I had heard the chorus sung at a service, and it made an impression on my heart. I must have fallen asleep when Jesus revealed Himself to me. It had happened on February 26, 2015.

24

In my dream, an extremely "in awe" moment, I was looking outside a window gazing at the formations of clouds in the sky. My heart said, it was of the mighty works of God, as the Lord was displaying pictures in the heaven. In my amazement, it seemed as though the clouds were appearing as many faces. It looked like the lion, the lamb and many other animals. Suddenly, I saw angels with flicking lights as the face of a man appeared. The pictures were changing constantly and there appeared a face of a bear, a face of a lion and so on, I was mesmerized. I thought it would be good to let Esther and Benjamin two kids I loved, come outside of the building to see the beautiful formations in the sky.

We seemed to be at a seaport wharf. I felt like I should go outside to the shore and have a better view of the sky. Cloud watching was one of my hobbies. As the clouds were still forming different images, I went to get the kids, and we came outside. I let them climb to the roof of the building to see the sky better. As they began to climb the stairs up to what seemed like a viewing gallery so they could have a clear look. I saw Him – Jesus's face.

He kept appearing to me in the clouds. I turned to my right side to look, and I saw Him come upon the earth, as He began to walk towards me.

Jesus had come a few feet from me. He was dressed in a linen wrap around his loins. He was a young Jewish man, in his thirties and very healthy and strong in appearance. He was very fair, His face had a neatly groomed beard; He was very handsome and physically well-shaped. His eyes were light colored, as they were eyes of love. His wavy hair was shoulder length and it was dripping wet. As He lifted His right arm up to show me His strength, it was amazing, very muscular like the strength of an athlete. I stood there frozen, as He demonstrated His strength with His right arm. He began to remove the sand with a twig from a branch to make a path or trench for water to flow. The twig was functioning as a heavy duty spade or shovel at work. My heart told me that He was just preforming His duty. He did not say a word; nevertheless, my heart understood His love for me.

There was a female security guard at the wharf post and I tried to inquire of her, if she had seen him too. I was so excited; I woke myself up with my loud 'WOW' as I fell off my bed and onto the floor.

I felt my heart ache, as I said, 'I Love You Jesus – I want more of you Jesus!'

I shouted, 'Holy Ghost' as I got up and looked outside. There was snow pouring down heavily almost like heavenly purified water.
The revelation of this experience had this meaning - there is a battle line drawn, as Jesus drew the line in the form of a trench or pathway of separation to two sides. When you desire an encounter with the Lord God, He will come into your atmosphere and surround you with His love and favor. No one or nothing can stop God's divine presence.

Chapter Six

A Picture to Behold Jesus

"I even, I Am the Lord, and besides me there is no savior."
Isaiah 43:11

After this encounter with the Lord Jesus, I had pondered what He had revealed to me. A few days after the encounter I had, the Holy Spirit prompted me to study the right arm of God. In obedience I began a venture to find all the powerful characteristics of the right arm of the Lord. As I began to record in my notebook the scripture of the Lord's right arm, the Holy Spirit brought this scripture to my mind.

"I the Lord have called thee in righteousness, and will hold thine hand, and
will keep thee, and give thee a covenant of the people for a light to the
Gentiles; to open the blind eyes, to bring out the prisoners from the prison,
and them that sit in darkness out of the prison house."
Isaiah 42:6-7

One day I received a nudge in my spirit to continue studying all the parts of the Lord as it related to a man. It began a desire in me to inquire of every scripture pertaining to the person of the Lord in reference to what the Bible had said of Him from His head to His feet.

I became aware that the Holy Spirit was actively involved in my quest for the truth. At different times He brought many scriptures into my remembrance and they were precisely for a particular topic I had to record on that occasion. I must pause to acknowledge the Holy Ghost as I would never be able to give Him a sufficient 'Thank you!' He is indeed the greatest teacher I would ever know.

The many attributes of Jesus's nature will overwhelm your imagination as each revelation of the picture frame of truth was completely adapted from the scriptures. These topics are meant to intrigue and propel you to a closer relationship with the Lord Jesus Christ.

JESUS IS BEAUTIFUL!

He is beautiful in appearance. Jesus is Jewish and a very handsome man as I got a glimpse personally of His humanity. I am aware that most of the accounts of His appearances found in the bible were in His glorious formation and with that in mind I do recommend you desire a personal encounter.

The bible has taken into account some references of what Jesus looked like in resemblance to the Father God. He was born in Bethlehem in the city of David. The details to be found of Jesus were that he was of Jewish descent (Matthew 1:17-18). It was declared that out of the lineage of King David a savior was born known to the Jews as Jesus or 'Yeshua.'

The description given of King David, according to the Bible was that he was a beautiful man. David was described as a ruddy-red and he had a beautiful countenance, he was of a fair complexion, with eyes to gaze upon, and of an exceptional type of beauty (1 Samuel: 16:12).

The scriptures also said that David's son Absalom was a beauty from the crown of his head to the sole of his feet; there was no blemish in him. He was fair and he had a beautiful head of hair, that every year end he had to cut his hair to keep it groomed (2 Samuel 14:25).

Can you grasp the concept? Jesus was called the Son of David! Their generational heritage was potentially of a beautiful countenance in their family tree.

Jesus had radiated beauty on the outside in conclusion and according to the scriptures He was internally beautiful also, as the Son of God for He had no unrighteousness in Him (Psalm 92:15).

"For God commanded the light to shine out of darkness, hath shined in our hearts, to give the light of knowledge of the glory of God in the face of Jesus Christ."
2Corinthians 4:6

HIS HAIR

When Jesus approached me, I saw that His hair was of a hazel-brown color upon His head. It seemed wavy at his shoulder length. Funny to imagine, but to be clear Jesus was not bald headed. Daniel revealed that he saw the Lord with hair as pure as wool (Daniel 7:9). The Lord was in his glorious appearance. In the book of revelation John the revelator saw the Lord as he appeared hairy. It sounded similar to the picture given of David's son Absalom.

"His head and his hairs were white like wool."
Revelation 1:14

HIS FACE

His face was of a fair complexion and expressed love. He also had neatly groomed beard. His countenance was penetrated gaze of love and compassion. He radiated light that captivated my heart with unlimited love and fulfilment. Jesus's face will captivate the hearts of everyone that encounters Him. I have heard testimonies of people who have the same experience.

God is inviting us to have an encounter with Him and to be a reflection of God's face in our looks. We will become what we behold. The Lord had commanded Moses to have his brother Aaron to say a Priestly blessing over the people. Even today, the Jewish Priest pronounces that blessings as they assemble over God's people.

"The Lord makes his face to shine upon you and be gracious to you."
Numbers 6:25

HIS EYES

Jesus's eyes are like a light bluish-color; a reflection of the sea. His eyes had a fixed gaze and an intense look of love and desire to commune with me. They pierced straight through my heart and I felt unworthy and transparent. Nothing was hidden from Him, nevertheless His stare was one of compassion and understanding of my need for Him.

The purest description of his eyes is written in the Songs of Songs. The scripture declared, His eyes are likened to Doves' eyes. A scientific explanation of these types of eyes is: they are fixed and do not move around in the socket; the dove's eyes have a penetrating gaze.

"I will instruct thee and teach thee in the way which thou shalt go: I will guide thee with mine eye."
Psalms 32:8

The scripture declared, *"The eyes of the Lord are in every place, beholding the good and the evil"* (Proverbs 15:3). This lets us know that there is nothing hidden from the Lord. Jesus sees the plans and schemes of the wicked against His people as they plot to destroy them.

"For the eyes of the Lord run to and fro through the whole earth, to shew Himself strong in the behalf of them whose heart is perfect towards Him."
2 Chronicles 16:9

HIS EYELIDS

There is one mention of Jesus's eyelids in reference to His power in the bible. This is self-explicit as the bible said that His eyelids tried the children of men. This meant that men would be tested or examined of their characters and demeanor by the Lord's eyelids; and their cases will be tried and judged according to His justice.

One morning in prayer the Holy Ghost led me to this scripture in Psalms. He knew my curiosity to search out the truth and as my teacher He had gave me this as a bonus. Thank you, Holy Ghost!

"The Lord is in his holy temple, the Lord's throne is in the heaven: His eyes behold, His eyelids try the children of men."
Psalm 11:4

HIS EARS

Can you imagine the Lord's ears are so huge, that He hears the cries of the whole earth? He hears the prayers of the saints and the cries of the little ones.

31

The Bible declares that *His ear is not heavy, that it cannot hear* (Isaiah 59:1).

"The Lord heard the cries of the lad, Ishmael when his mom Hagar she ran out of water and placed him under the shrubs to die, in the book of Genesis. And God heard the voice of the lad; and the angel of called to Hagar out of heaven."

Genesis 21:17

The Lord heard the repentant cries from the city of Nineveh. The scriptures stated that after Jonah brought the warning the people of Nineveh believed God and proclaimed a fast, as they put on sackcloth from the greatest of them even to the least of them. And God saw their works that they turned from their evil way; and God repented of the evil, that He had said he would do unto them, and he did not (Jonah 3:7-10).

"Thank you Lord, for your ears are not too small to hear the faintest cries. In my anguish, I cried out to you for help, and you heard me and rescued me, so I could tell others of your amazing mercies."

HIS MOUTH

The Lord's mouth is powerful. It brings forth thunder and lightning to declare His majesty. When the Lord speaks it will not return to Him empty without accomplishing what He desired (Isaiah 55:11).

The Bible declared, in the ancient times that many godly men served as spokesmen for the Lord as He used their mouths to speak in his authority.

Jesus rebuts the Devil's temptation by quoting the scripture; *"Man shall not live by bread alone, but by every word that proceed out of the mouth of God"* (Deuteronomy 8:3).

"For the Lord giveth wisdom: out of his mouth cometh knowledge and understanding."
Proverbs 2: 6

All our victory belongs to Jesus. I recall that someone mentioned to me that victory has a big mouth. Death is swallowed up in victory. I believe all types of cancer and diabetes, all sicknesses and diseases that are responsible for death were swallowed up in victory.

The scriptures declared, *"But thanks be to God, which giveth us victory through our Lord Jesus Christ"* (1 Corinthians 15:57).

HIS VOICE

"The Voice of the Lord is powerful; the voice of the Lord is majesty."
Psalm 29:4

I realized that there is a difference between the voice of Jesus and the voice of the Father. The Lord Jesus has an audible voice. His voice is sweet and gentle and has more of a melodious tone. Whereas, the Father has a thunderous voice that sound and feels like vibrations that penetrate the soul.

You can experience both voices with the grace of God. I cannot describe in words an encounter with the Father nor could prepare anyone for Him. My explanation was mild and I learned that he speaks through the Holy Ghost most of the time so as not to make us overwhelmed.

"The voice of the Lord is upon the waters: The God of glory thundereth."
Psalms 29:3

HIS BOSOM

The scripture declared that the Lord revealed Himself as *El Shaddai*. These words in Hebrew primarily mean, *"Breasted One,"* which was formed from the root word *'Shad,'* which means *'the breast.'*

The Lord is the Mighty One with an udder, as a mother who produces milk. In another verse the Lord is likened to a hen that gathers her brood under her wings (Luke 13:34). This illustrates how the chicks were under her breast in a secure place.

"He shall feed his flock like a shepherd, he shall gather the lambs in his arm, and carry them in his bosom."
Isaiah 40:11

HIS HEART

Jesus's heart is full of love and compassion. The sacrifice of his life was an indication of how much his heart is towards His people. As a loving Father he pursues the lost. His desire is that none should perish, but all should come to repentance.

With His heart of love the Lord God came looking for Adam and Eve as they hid themselves. He knew they had sinned and were afraid, yet He came looking for them. As a compassionate Lord, He knew their frames were made of the dirt (Psalm 103:14).

Jesus comes looking for you in your messed-up conditions, as you are far away from Him. His compassion flows out of a heart of love to see you walk in victory.

"Unto Adam and his wife did the Lord make coats of skin and clothed them."
Genesis 3:21

"For God so loved the world, that he gave his begotten Son, that whosoever believeth in Him should not perish but have everlasting life."
John 3:16

"He knew that they were but flesh; a wind that passeth away, and cometh not again."
Psalm 78:39

HIS GRIEVED HEART

The Lord is grieved in His heart at times. You must recognize this is an attribute of his personality. The bible declares that Jesus left His divinity and He took on humanity in order to share with our emotions as He dwelled among us.

Jesus finds no pleasure in the sinful man and seems grieved by their rebellion. He is truly grieved as people do evil against the Lord and other people.

"And God saw that the wickedness of man was great in the earth, and that every imagination of their thoughts of his heart was only evil continually. And it repented the Lord that he had made man on the earth, and it grieved him at his heart."
Genesis 6:5-6

HIS RIGHT ARM

The Right Arm of the Lord is full of strength and power. He portrays so much power that He moves mountains that stand in his way, how about that?

He can move any mighty mountain that stands in your way as well. In Moses episode of the Exodus of the Jews, the Lord God parted the red sea with His right arm, which demonstrated His awesome power. The prophet Isaiah declared, *'Behold, the Lord will come with a strong hand, and his arm shall rule for him'* (Isaiah 40:11).

"The eternal God is thy refuge, and underneath are the everlasting arms: and he shall thrust out the enemy from before thee, and shall say 'Destroy them.'"
Deuteronomy 33:27

HIS HANDS

The hands of the Lord God are so powerful and huge so much so that the whole world is held in His hands. I cannot comprehend with my imaginary mind the extent of his nature or fathom my little stature in His hands. I might be just a speck of dust in His hands.

The Hebrew sages stated that when God created the animals He used one hand, but when He created the man Adam, He personally and intimately used His two hands. You will not see this in the English, but in the Hebrew writings it was shown that the word *"Yod"* meaning hand was repeated twice in the verse (Genesis 2:7-8).

In consideration of His hands, I pictured the Lord holding the young ones and the old ones, the little tiny babies and the children in His hands. He holds the rich and the poor, the needy and the sick ones. Besides, He has all who are healthy in His hands and in those hands, God holds the sinners and the saints.

"Behold the Hand of the Lord is not shortened, that it cannot save, neither his ears heavy, that it cannot hear."
Isaiah 59:1

"Thy hands have made me and fashioned me: give me understanding, that I may learn thy commandments."
Psalms 119:73

His Finger

The finger is the second smallest limb of the body. The Lord used His finger for creative miracles. The Lord used His fingers to write the two tablets that He gave to Moses at Mount Sinai (Exodus 8:19).

The finger of the Lord casting out devils was an illustration of His strength and power. God used His finger to write upon the wall of King Belshazzar's feast because of the King's abomination of the Temple vessels (Daniel 5).

At the feast celebrations, the Lord required the priest to use His finger to sprinkle the blood of the lamb seven times at the altar as a foreshadow of Jesus' crucifixion. Jesus did shed His blood in seven places from the trail to His death (Isaiah 53:5-7).

"When I Consider thy heavens, the work of thy fingers, the moon and the stars, which thou hast ordained."
Psalm 8:3

"Then the magicians said unto Pharaoh, 'This is the finger of God: and Pharaoh's heart hardened.'"
Exodus 8:19

HIS SHOULDER

The word *"Massa"* in the Hebrew means *"to be a burden bearer."* In the scriptures Jesus said, "Come unto to me, all ye that labour and are heavy laden, and I will give you rest."

The Lord extended such an invitation and I perceived that the Lord's shoulder is really wide and strong. This means He cannot be overloaded with all the cares and burdens of this world. Even yours and mine are not too heavy. This assures me that there is no sickness or sin; sadness or financial lack that my Lord did not carry. I am convinced even the anxiety and fear we have, Jesus carries upon his shoulder as well.

"For unto to us a child is born, to us a son is given; and the government will be upon His shoulder: 'Yeshua is his name!'"
Isaiah 9:6

"Cast your burden unto the Lord, (Shoulder) and he shall sustain thee: He shall never suffer the righteous to be moved."
Isaiah 55:22

HIS FEET

Great power was demonstrated by the feet of the Lord. Zachariah the prophet declared that he saw in a vision, as the Lord shall put his feet upon the top of the mountain of Zion in Israel, it will be parted into two on his return.

The Lord Jesus bruised the serpent's head (better known as Satan) under his feet and he became as dust.

"Thou hast put all things in subjection under his feet. For in that he put all in subjection under him, he left nothing that is not under him."
Hebrews 2:8

Chapter Seven

His Special Features

HIS SPECIAL FEATURES

"But when they came to Jesus, and saw that he was dead already, they broke not his legs: But one of the soldiers with a spear pierced his side, and forthwith came there out blood and water."
John 19:33-34

HIS SIDE

I was inspired to reveal His side as a very important feature in the continuation of my study of the person of Jesus Christ. The piercing of Jesus side was an answer to the soldiers' question, to ensure that Jesus was already dead. These things were done so that the scriptures would be fulfilled as it was noted that not a bone of Jesus would be broken. God had instructed Moses not to break the leg of the lamb during the atonement. This was a foreshadow of the Lamb of the Passover as Jesus is the sacrificial lamb (Number 9:12).

"He was wounded for our transgressions, he was bruised for our iniquities; the chastisement of our peace was upon him; and with his stripes we are healed."
Isaiah 53:5

The Hebrew scholars said the water and the blood that came out of Jesus's side signified the natural and the spiritual death. In a similar fashion it could have represented the flesh as the blood and the Spirit as the water flowed. Another theory suggests that the blood of Jesus took away our sins, and the water that flowed out of His side took away our spiritual death.

The bible said, *"These things were written that you might believe that Jesus is the Christ, the Son of God; and that believing you might have life through his name"* (John 20:31).

HIS SPIRIT

"The Lord is that spirit: and where the spirit of the Lord is there is liberty."
2 Cor 3: 17

The spirit of the Lord is His personality; He communes with us in a gentle voice. The essence of God's power is the Holy Spirit, as the Spirit executes the plans and commands of the Father God. The Holy Spirit is a comforter and supernatural power to all who trust in God.

The Holy Spirit has many other functions, as he gives gifts and testifies of the Lord. He is a teacher and a guide into all truth (John 16:13). He reproves of sin and of righteousness, and of judgement (John 16:8). He can be grieved or be vexed (Ephesians 4:30). The Spirit of the Lord has constant movement as He speaks and guides us. You have to learn how to let the presence of the Holy Spirit stay with you.

The bible declared, the Spirit of God moved upon the face of the waters (Genesis 1:2). Jesus said, "I am the living water." The Holy Spirit is represented as the living water.

The way to walk with the Spirit of the Lord God is simple. The key to receiving the Holy Spirit is to invite Him into your heart, and believe by faith in prayer that you have received him. You will experience His presence and through this encounter you will begin to receive revelation, knowledge and understanding of the person of Jesus Christ.

"The Comforter, which is the Holy Ghost, whom the Father will send in my name, He shall teach you all things."
John 14:26

"Seek ye the Lord while he may be found, call ye upon him while he is near: let the wicked forsake his way, and the unrighteous man his thoughts: and let him return unto the Lord, and he will have mercy upon him; and to our God, for he will pardon."
Isaiah 55:6-7

HIS BLOOD

There is power in the blood of Jesus! The blood of Jesus will never lose its power!

The blood of Jesus is the cleansing power for every sin and iniquity in our life. God the Father sacrificed His only begotten son. Jesus came in human flesh to the earth and bought us back to the father by His blood. Through Jesus blood that was shed at the cross on Calvary, His burial, and His resurrection you have victory and deliverance to overcome evil.

The scriptures declare that the blood of bulls and goats, and the ashes of a heifer could not purify the soul (Hebrew 9:13). In the Old

Testament the blood of the sacrificed animal was sprinkled seven times around the altar of the Tabernacle, as a foreshadow of the seven times Jesus shed His blood as He endured the cross. Only the Blood of Jesus could cleanse sins. It is the blood of Jesus that conquers all the wickedness surrounding you. The devil is afraid of the precious blood of Jesus Christ.

The bible declares that man was born in sin and formed in iniquities (Romans 5:12). By accepting Jesus Christ as your Lord and savior you can receive forgiveness through his blood from all unrighteousness. By exchanging your generational DNA with the DNA of Jesus, His blood is now flowing through your veins and it flushes out all of your iniquities and sin. Inviting the Lord Jesus as your personal savior is evident as the Holy Spirit does a quick work to bring you into the freedom of His love.

"Having therefore, brethren, boldness to enter into the holiest by the blood of Jesus, by a new and living way, which he hath consecrated for us, through the veil, that is to say, his flesh."
Hebrew 10:19-2

"Therefore, just as through one-man sin entered into the world, death through sin, and so death spread to all men."
Roman 5:12

THE CRUCIFIXION SCENE

It was in the middle of December 2017, as everyone began preparations for Christmas celebrations. I was not excited much for the season just yet, when I had a dream.

I was standing on a high mountain that seemed like a tourist sight. At that moment I was looking up into the sky; it was a cloudy day. Below the dense clouds there were a few small grey clouds in a formation which attracted my attention, as I wondered why they were separate from the rest of the clouds. They seemed sort of inter-twined and as I kept staring, they began to separate from each other.

Suddenly, Jesus appeared in the midst of the small clouds. He was dressed in his loin-cloth with his hand bound and his feet bound. He looked fragile, as he was suspended helpless while soldiers beat him. They began violently fighting, tearing at His body, like the powers of darkness were forcing them. I started to yell out for people who were on the mountain to look up into the sky and see what they were doing to Jesus the Lord.

I called for some children I thought were on the tour but the ones I knew were not nearby, so I told a little girl to come quickly and get them. As I yelled out everyone present began to look up in silence as the crucifixion of Jesus was being displayed in the sky. There were two women who appeared on the scene and inquired as to what was happening. I was annoyed that they did not care enough to look up and see what we were gazing at the way the Lord suffered for our redemption.

I woke up shaken as I found myself crying for those that are lost, that they may find Christ in this Christmas season. I pray that all may behold you Jesus and turn to you as Lord and Savior. Thank you, Lord, for the revelation of your crucifixion, in Jesus Name.

There is truth in the birth of the Lord Jesus which most people celebrate during the Christmas season. The story of Jesus's birth is only significant in relation to His sacrificial death (Mark 8:27-33). We have to realize that Jesus was born to die (Hebrews 10:5-7). The manger scene led directly to the Cross.

The scriptures declared, that God so loved the world that He gave His only begotten Son (John 3:16). It is important to remember that Jesus was born to die for our sins, and to make us right with God. He was raised from the dead to vindicate the righteousness of God (1 Corinthians 15:3-5).

His birth was also the beginning step towards His sacrifice for our deliverance (Hebrews 2:9-18). The Lord who left divinity took upon Himself humanity in order to die as our sin offering before the Father God.

Chapter Eight

His Personality Explored

"Arise and shine; for thy light is come and the glory of the Lord is risen upon thee."
Isaiah 60:1

Have you ever stopped to consider, is Jesus really a person? Can you visualize Jesus's personality as he breathes, His heart beats, He sees everything, He moves and speaks. He has thoughts and He expresses emotions: whether happiness and sadness, and He occasionally expresses anger?

He is really an awesome God. There are many scriptures to describe the Lord Jesus in His nature and character. I would encourage you, to be zealous to see the Lord in different facets. Moreover, I will share a few of my experiences with the Lord, as a means to stir your appetite to know Him personally. My prayer for you is that you will meet the same Lord Jesus and to have awesome experiences, in Jesus name.

HE MOVES

Jesus was referred to the source of living water. I beckon to differ and say Jesus was not stagnant. His incomprehensible power to move in the heavens, on the earth and under the earth when He had needed is a mystery. The bible declared that the Lord's movement was in the midst of the cloud as he led the people in the wilderness (Exodus 40:36-38).

According to the bible, through the Holy Spirit, Jesus has access to our lives. His spirit lives inside of me and can live in you too. There is no movement without our spirit, for it is God's spirit that gives us life. Therefore, as the Spirit of God lives inside of you whenever you move, He will move also. This is something to consider.

It is not frequently taught to the believer, how easily the Lord and the Holy Spirit would drifts away in times when He felt grieved. Therefore, you should be conscious of the presence of the Lord at all times, just as we have relationships with each other and we try to avoid conflicts and offense.

King David had the revelation of the movement of the Spirit of the Lord as he recognized that God had seen all his sins. The Lord sent the prophet Nathan to ask of David what judgement he would preferred as a consequence of his sins. David declared, there is nowhere to hide from the Holy Ghost, where He cannot hide from us (2 Samuel 12:1-7).

"Whither shall I go from thy spirit? Or whither shall I flee from thy presence."
Psalm 139:7

In many instances the bible declares that the Spirit of the Lord picks God's servants up or rests upon them. In one story the Lord visited Ezekiel and told him that His Spirit would empower him to do the

Lord's will. This means the spirit of God will empower you to do His will also.

"And I will put my spirit within you, and cause you to walk in my statues, and ye shall keep my judgements, and do them."
Ezekiel 36:27

HE HIDES

Did you know that the Lord has a hobby? The answer is yes! The Lord's favorite game is 'Hide and Seek.'

The Holy Ghost revealed this to me. In this game you have a part to play. Jesus wants you to seek him, as He hides. The bible declares that the Lord hides and withdraws as He loves for you to seek him in prayer.

The Bible declares, "The Lord God hides from all unrighteousness" (Isaiah 59:2). This means: The withdrawal of the Divine presence himself as a result of all sin.

Our selfish desire causes the Lord to hide His face from us. Whenever you remove yourself from the truth of His presence it causes evil to blind you. You should be mindful of the content of your heart as it could cause the Lord's divine presence to be removed from you.

The Holy Ghost's presence quietly drifts away without announcement from those that grieve His spirit. He hides just like the Lord God hides.

King Saul was a prime example of the reason the Lord hides. Saul became proud and disobedient to the man of God which resulted in him being dethroned by the Lord. The bible declares: After the death of the prophet Samuel, King Saul's demise was of rebellion to God as he consulted with the wizard and brought judgement to his household.

This lesson was about Jesus Christ as the Shepherd and King. As the Shunamite woman in the Song of Songs, because of her neglect to the Lord, she lost His presence. She had to endure much hardship, as she was beaten and wounded by the watchmen and embarrassed by the keepers of the wall, before she found him again. Her neglect of the shepherd's presence caused her to experience the sufferings of evil men. Her story changed at the end as she surrendered her will and she found the Shepherd. The story is relevant to the way God would allow some things to happen in our life for a period of time, so that he can get our attention.

"I opened to my beloved; but my beloved had withdrawn himself, and was gone: my soul failed when he spake: I sought him, but I could not find him; I called him, but he gave me no answer."
Song of Songs 5:6

King David pleaded for the Lord to not forsake him after he sinned with Bathsheba and the planned for her husband Uriah's death. He felt that the Lord would not return to the sweet fellowship they once had. David pleads for the Lord's presence and mercy and as a result of the restoration of their friendship and love; it then resulted in a covenant of Jesus Christ becoming the son of David.

"How long wilt thou forget me, O Lord? Forever? How long wilt thou hide thy face from me?"
Psalm 13:1

In the story of Job's dilemma, he recognized that the Lord was absent when he needed Him the most. Job didn't know that Satan was given permission for a period of time to test him. Job felt the Lord was hiding His face from him (Job 13:24).

There were pleas from the priest of ancient days as they entered into captivity as a result of the sins of their nation. And the Lord declared that He was going to hide His face in the time of their calamities.

"Wherefore hidest thou thy face, and forgettest our affliction and our oppression?"
Psalm 44:24

HIS METICULOUS WAYS

The Lord God was meticulous in many ways, 'Who can be compared with Him?'

Many facets of Jesus's mannerisms were recognizable as the scriptures identified them clearly. In the book of Leviticus many of his peculiar ways are revealed.

I was amused at how fastidious the Lord was in the book of Leviticus. The Lord told Moses of His standard requirement concerning the Tabernacle operations. According to the Lord's descriptions the work of the Holy place was to be accomplished by only certain chosen priests. When it came to the Holy of Holies it was exceptional. The Lord required, 'None with blemish nor lame could enter the Holy place.'

The Lord would graciously allow every priest to do work in the house of the Lord. They could attend to the sacrifices and the cleaning of the Tabernacle, outside the Holy place, it was their boundary line.

His commands regarding the type of animals were of a certain year and condition for making the atonement sacrifice. 'None Blemished!' Jesus was so peculiar even in accepting our gifts (Leviticus 22). The Lord had an issue with the Priest of the Tabernacle and He cautioned them for allowing the people to bring any type of sacrifices that polluted the table (Malachi 1:12-13).

At the dedication of the Tabernacle the Lord also spoke to Moses concerning the way the Priest should not dissect the poor persons offering of the pigeon and turtle doves. He wanted it offered up whole so it looked like much in their sight (Leviticus1: 15-17).

I realized that the Lord was a skilled chef. He had exquisite taste according to the recipes he requested of flour, oil and frankincense for his cakes with his meat offering. He loved his meat seasoned with salt and the grains flavored with oil. Can you imagine that the Lord loves fried food? (Leviticus 1-3).

I found this amusing and at the same time familiar, as the Lord God had his preferences too. I have considered my attitude towards vegetables and fruits. The pickiness of my nature pertaining to these items is validated. It is funny that I always refuse to eat anything that is bruised or speckled. Do you find yourself with similar behavioral patterns?

Chapter Nine

His Nature

HIS EMOTIONS

Except in His governmental authority as He also possesses a divine nature; Jesus' characteristics transcend the earthly environment which you as a human operate within. Jesus took on human flesh in order to share with your emotions. He had happiness and was fulfilled as He willingly died in your place; for sins He had not committed in order to bring you to His promise of Redemption.

"Looking unto the Jesus the author and finisher of our faith; who for the joy that was set before him endured the cross, despising the shame, and sat down at the right hand of the throne of God."
Hebrew 12:2

Jesus' circumstances of life on the earth were similar to yours today in many ways. He experienced situations of sadness that made him weep. The bible said, Jesus wept over the city of Jerusalem and He wept for the death of Lazarus.

At times He showed emotions of happiness. The bible declared that He was happy to see people whose souls were lost, saved. He loved the children around him, as they make joyful events and memories of happiness. In His nature, the Lord is exceedingly compassionate. Jesus was touched with every feeling of infirmity, this meant He had similar emotions like mankind (Hebrews 4:15).

"Let him that glorieth glory in this, that he understandeth and knoweth me, that I am the Lord which exercise loving kindness, judgement, and righteousness, in the earth: for in these things I delight, saith the Lord."
Jeremiah 9:24

HIS HUMILITY

Jesus was known as a man of humility. His obedience to the Father was a great example of the character of our Savior Jesus Christ. He was as humble as a Lamb in obedience to the cross for your sins and mine (Philippians 2:8).

Jesus taught the people, 'Blessed are the poor in spirit: for theirs is the kingdom of heaven' (Matthew 5:3). The Psalmist David declared, 'The meek shall inherit the earth; and shall delight themselves in the abundance of peace.' (Psalm 37:11). Lord, help us to humble ourselves.

Jesus was much gentler than his Father God in comparison of their characters. The bible summarized the Lord Jesus revealed himself to Moses as the Holy One: full of righteousness, merciful, loving and kind, humble and compassionate (Exodus 34:6-7).

His generosity to humble himself and wash His disciples' feet illustrated His servant-spirit. As a believer you should examine your motives for servanthood.

"He riseth from supper, and took a towel, and girded himself. After that he poureth water into a basin, and began to wash the disciples' feet and wipe them with the towel."
John 13:4-5

"He was oppressed, and he was afflicted, yet he opened not his mouth: He is brought as a lamb to the slaughter, and as a sheep before shearers is dumb, so he openeth not his mouth."
Isaiah 53:7

"Though he were a son, yet learned he obedience by the things which he suffered. Being made perfect, he became the author of eternal salvation unto all them that obey him."
Hebrews 5:8-9

THE LORD LAUGHS

"He that sitteth in the heavens shall laugh."
Psalm 2:4

The Lord is very humorous, and this is something we as Christian believers miss out on. This is one of the reasons we must seek His face and read His word.

There were many humorous things written in the bible. As the word comes alive your imagination can visualize Jesus skipping and dancing in confidence like King David danced after His victory. He smiled and laughed just as we do and He also finds children very amusing just like we do. The bible declares that, He cautioned His disciples not to send the children away from Him (Luke 18:16). He laughs when we are happy and He is sad when we are hurt.

Jesus demonstrated happiness over the lost sheep that were found (Luke 15:5). He rejoiced as He anticipated His victory over Satan (Luke 10:21). The bible noted that when the evil ones' plot for the demise of the righteous the Lord would let them pay for their crimes. He would laugh at their calamity. The Lord declared through the prophets to Israel that He was not going to hear a people that were rebellious and forsook God.

"The wicked plotteth against the just, and gnasheth upon him with his teeth. The Lord shall laugh at him: for he seeth that his day is coming."
Psalm 37:12-13

HIS FUNNY HUMOR

I used to watch the soap operas, but decided it was becoming too immoral for my taste. One day as I was reading the story of Jacob's life and journey in the book of Genesis, I heard the Lord clearly as he spoke and said, 'The soap opera you like to watch was originated right here in the word of God.' As I continued to read, there I saw the revelation. The dramatic story of Jacob, Rachel, Leah and their two maids came alive as a modern day 'Soap Opera'. It was so amusing; I recommend you read the story (Genesis 29-30).

On another occasion, I was reading the book of Exodus concerning the story of Moses going up to Mount Sinai for forty days and forty nights to receive the Ten Commandments.' I heard the Lord whisper, 'Do you know how the doctors got the prescription of two tablets per dose.' I understood the terminology as a medical remedy but I was astonished, as I heard him continue, 'When Moses looked down and saw what the people had done, as they had made a Golden Calf as a way of rebellion against God, he instantly got a headache and had to take two tablets.' I found this to be very hilarious.

"Thou shall have no other gods before me."
Exodus 20:3

I found this amusing as I imagine the Lord had the last laugh. The priest and leaders who were pleased of the crucifixion of Jesus thought it would be the end to the religious uproar. They could not stop the manifestation of the Holy presence of the Lord. For on the day of Pentecost as the men were gathered in the upper room the Holy Ghost sat upon them.

The bible declared that everyone present began to speak with other tongues as the Spirit gave them utterance. This news was noised abroad and the multitude came to see and was confounded, because every man heard them speak in his own language. And they were all amazed and marveled (Acts 2:6).

The bible is filled with many amazing stories such as the prophet Elijah who in panic thought he was the only prophet alive as he ran from Jezebel. He pleaded for his life as the Lord told him to get himself together because He had seven thousand prophets besides him to do His work (1 Kings 19:18).

How about the story of Jonah who had built himself a sukkot or tent to wait out the judgement of God for Nineveh? While he waited the Lord prepared a gourd to give him shade over his head, and to deliver him from his grief. The bible said, and so Jonah was glad for the gourd. But it came to pass when morning rose the Lord prepared a worm to puncture the gourd and it withered up. Then the sun arose and the Lord prepared a vehement wind; and the sun beat upon his head until he fainted (Jonah 4).

HIS HILARIOUS FINGER

As I was writing these stories the Holy Spirit reminded me of a scary story of the bible. The king Belshazzar made a great feast and he commanded his servants to bring the vessels of the temple of God to drink from. The bible said, and the same hour they drank as they praised the gods of gold and of silver.

There appeared fingers of a man's hand and wrote over against the candlestick upon the plaster of the wall in his palace: and the King saw the part of the hand that wrote. I find that to be very eerie and scary, reminding me of Halloween pranks. In essence the Lord is the best pranker in the world. The scriptures declare that God created good and evil. I propose this could be the way they fostered Halloween and I find this to be so amusing.

The story concluded by describing the response of the King. Could you imagine the king's face? *"His countenance changed and his thoughts troubled him, so that the joints of his loins became loosed, and his knees smote one against another. As he cried aloud to bring all the soothsayers and astrologers but no one could not read nor interpret the writing"* (Daniel 5:1-8).

"I also will laugh at your calamity; I will mock when your fear cometh."
Proverbs 1:26

Chapter Ten

His Faithfulness

"If we believe not, yet he abide faithful: he cannot deny himself."
2 Timothy 2: 13

The Lord is well known for his integrity which is recognizable in your life. His faithfulness had been proven over and over again in the Word of God as we see His word is true. The bible declares that, God cannot lie, nor can He break His covenant promises (Hebrew 6:18). Every covenant fulfilled and every promise foretold has and will come true. Testimony after testimony of God's faithfulness was found through the bible, of people who have given testimony and even by people today.

Throughout the relationship with the Hebrew people there is evidence of the Lord's faithfulness. God made a covenant with Abraham and has fulfilled it as He promised Abraham that he would be a patriarch of many nations. Though the people were scattered because of rebellion, the Lord had promised they would return to their land. Today this is fulfilled (Zachariah 8:7-8).

The Lord is always faithful even in times of your disobedience. He loves you despite your faults. It is the Lord's mercies that we are not consumed, because His compassions fail not. They are new every morning: great is thy faithfulness (Lamentations 3:22-23).

"If we confess our sins, he is faithful and just to forgive us our sins, and to cleanse us from all unrighteousness."
1 John 1:9

"The Lord is not slack concerning His promise, as some men count slackness; but is longsuffering to us-ward, not willing that any should perish, but that all should come to repentance."
2 Peter 3:9

HIS THOUGHTS

We cannot place an adjective to the Lord's nature of love (Luke 22:32). Our wellbeing is His priority as we are always on Jesus's mind. The Lord never takes time out of his busy schedule; he is always at your beck and call. He is an amazing God as His original plan was for you to worship and dwell with Him. The bible says, the Lord comes to reset things when you are asleep (Psalms 16:7). I will bless the Lord, who hath given me counsel: my reins also instruct me in the night season.

The scriptures say Jesus makes intercession for us as our High Priest. It is not complicated! As illustrated, he constantly prays for our salvation, as He prayed for the apostle Peter in his time of temptation.

The psalmist stated:

"How precious are thy thoughts unto me! O God! How great is the sum of them! Indescribable and incomprehensible might be the closest explanation of who the Lord is. In thy book – you wrote all your thoughts concerning my destiny. Thine eyes did see my substance, yet being unperfect; in thy book, all my members were written, which in continuance were fashioned, when as yet there was none of them"
(Psalm 139:16- 17).

"For I know the thoughts that I think toward you, saith the Lord, thoughts of peace, and not of evil, to give you an expected end."
(Jeremiah 29:11)

HIS QUESTIONS

Do you realize that the Lord Jesus has questions too? The answer is yes! One of his personality traits shows that the Lord had many questions of his own.

"For the Lord hath a controversy with his people, and he plead with Israel. O my people, what have I done unto thee? And wherein have I wearied thee? Testify against me."
Micah 6:2-3

I am positive you have a few questions for the Lord, too. The scriptures imply that by nature you would have questions. This amazing knowledge was revealed to me out of communing with the Lord. He oft times asks questions and gives you the answers in the clarifications to many of those questions. In Genesis the Lord asked Cain for his brother Abel to hear what he would say (Genesis 4:9).

"And the Lord God called unto Adam, and said unto him, 'Where art thou?' and 'Who told thee that thou was naked?'"
Genesis 3:9-10

The Lord Jesus understands you have a tendency to need to know the basics. It is very brave to ask questions of the Lord as you often speak out aloud the thoughts you have concerning events in your life, especially those which you felt that God could have prevented from happening.

I plead guilty for asking questions: 'Why Lord, Why me, Not again?'

The bible said that Jesus asked his father to remove the cup of suffering from him. On the Mount of Olives before his crucifixion, Jesus had a moment in his human state at that Place. The mystery of that place was of significance, and Jesus understood the meaning.

In Jewish culture the Mount of Olives is known as the place of crushing. It was where the Jews crushed and bruised the olive fruits in order to produce olive oil. Jesus understood that He would experience great suffering and perhaps He asked for a change of plans.

I believe it was there that Jesus saw the revelation of the greater picture of the victory, as an angel of the Lord appeared from heaven and strengthened him for His task. He received confidence to conquer the devil, and prevail over sin and death. The bible says that, "There on that mount Jesus humbled himself in obedience to the cross" (Luke 22:41-43).

In our disgust and questions, the Lord can relate to our concerns for it is an attribute we have adapted from Him.

While reading the scriptures, I came across a conversation in the book of Job. It seemed that there was a pretty intense discussion between Job and the Lord. Job's murmuring caused the Lord to ask him some very difficult questions. This caused Job to become speechless as his pitiful mind had no reason to reply.

> *"Then the Lord answered Job out of the whirlwind, and said, 'Who, is this that darkeneth counsel by words, without knowledge?'"* And in another question, *'Where was thou, when I laid the foundations of the earth?'"* (Job 38:1-4).

Many other questions did the Lord pose to Job to prove His sovereignty in creation and that He was in control of Job's most difficult of situations.

In another incident the children of Israel were in rebellion as they continuously practiced offensive sins.

The Lord was very disgusted at their refusal to trust Him as their God. They were His chosen people and the bride of the Lord, so He asked for a bill of divorcement. The Lord continued by asking why they doubted His love.

"Thus, said the Lord, 'Where is the bill of your mother's divorcement, whom I put away?'"
Isaiah 50:1

"Can a woman forget her sucking child, that she should not have compassion on the son of her womb? Yea, they may forget, yet will I not forget thee. Behold I have graven thee upon the palms of my hands; thy walls are continually before me."
Isaiah 49:15

Chapter Eleven

God's Planned Seasons

HIS TIMES AND DATES

God is a Lord of time! He lives in eternity and He created time and things we cannot see. Time exists because the Lord has prepared a sequence of events in time so He can meet with us. All things function and operate in God's timing. We today lives in time not eternity.

A *Mo'edim* is a word in Hebrew meaning, "a set time." Nothing happens without the Lord God's sanction.

There are times within time: A time for favor, a time for judgement, a time for restoration, a time for blessings.

In the word of God, there was an appointed time and season for the birth of our Lord Jesus.

God has appointed times in a year; these were set dates and months. The Lord instructed Moses and his people to appear before him in the scriptures, at a particular season, three times a year. The children of Israel were required to all partake in these feasts days. They are the Feast of Passover, Feast of weeks or Pentecost, and the Feast of Tabernacles.

The Lord called them the times of refreshing, and the time for thanksgiving and remembrance. Israel under Moses leadership was commanded to acknowledge all the difficult times; to recall, and to remember all the Lord had delivered his people from (Exodus 12:14).

Consequently, a set time was given for the children of Israel in exile, which was for a length of seventy years.

The bible declared that, King Solomon offered burnt offerings unto the Lord on the altar of the Lord, which he built before the porch, even after a certain rate every day, offering according to the commandment of Moses, on the Sabbaths, and the new moons, and on the solemn feasts, three times in the year, even in the Feast of unleavened bread, and in the Feast of weeks (Pentecost), and in the Feasts of Tabernacles (2 Chronicles 8:12-13). It was many years after Moses, but today the people of Israel still adhere to Gods commands.

King David declared, "My times are in thy hand: deliver me from the hand of my enemies" (Psalm 31:15).

"Three times thou shalt keep a feast unto me in the year." (The Feast of Unleavened Bread, the Feast of Harvest and the Feast of Ingathering.) They are known in Hebrew as the Passover, Pentecost and Rosh Hashanah (Exodus 23:14-16).

"Daniel answered and said, "Blessed be the name of the God forever and ever: for wisdom and might is his: He change the times and seasons."
Daniel 2:20-21

The apostle Paul admonished the believers, to remember there is a time for Jesus return to the Earth.

'But of the times and seasons, brethren, ye have no need that I write to you. For yourselves know perfectly that the day of the Lord so cometh as a thief in the night.'

(1 Thessalonians 5:1-3)

As believers, you need to remember where Jesus has brought you from, and the many times He has delivered you from death and destruction, even though you didn't deserve it. It is fair to give thanks, for Him bringing us out of darkness into His marvelous Light.

THE REVELATION OF HIS BIRTH

In August of 2017 at 4 a.m. the Holy Ghost woke me up. When I awoke there was a song in my heart: 'You're a good, good Father!' He prompted me to go to the window and as I got up to take a look outside I was astonished to see a new moon above the window. As I returned to spend time in prayer suddenly, I heard the Holy Ghost in an audible voice say, 'Do you know what this moon means?'

I was in astonishment, as I replied, 'I don't, I know you definitely have an answer Lord.' In that moment he spoke again, 'This was the moon that Joseph and Mary followed back to Bethlehem, for Jesus to be born.' Then He continued to say, 'This was the reason why Jesus was born in the tent, for there was no place available in the Inn.' "Wow," I replied, as our fellowship concluded.

I was blown away as I had never heard anyone preach this revelation to my knowledge. This conversation amazed me; as I began to remember the season that we were in: it was the time of the Feast of Tabernacles. As a Jewish custom the people usually built tents outside their homes. This was a special appointed time commanded by the Lord God and the families kept it sacred annually. They would eat their meals under those tents as a thanksgiving and memorial of their deliverance from Egypt.

The scriptures declared that Jesus participated in these Feasts and was seen in the temple at a feast (John 5: 1). The Jewish scholars usually determine their seasons by the lunar of the moon according to God's design. The New Year celebrations called Rosh Hashanah was the beginning of their month of the Hebrew Calendar.

The Pharaoh understood the seasons and he understood their religious festivals. The Hebrew people yearly would always gather for an important event as this. Therefore, he knew it would be the appropriate time to do the census.

Abruptly I set out to search the New Testament books concerning Jesus's birth. The Holy Spirit was precise as I found in the writings of the apostle Luke account (Luke 2:1). I whispered, 'O Lord you are so amazing!' It was exactly the season of the Jewish Feast of Tabernacles that is known in Hebrew as Sukkot: The dwelling in booths or tents. This was an appointed time of God's Feast Days and a celebration of his birthday as he kept the feast.

"Ye shall dwell in booths seven days; all that are Israelites born shall dwell in booths: That your generations may know that I made the children of Israel to dwell in booth, when I brought them out of the land of Egypt: I AM the Lord."
Leviticus 23:24-43

The Circumstantial Events

The account of Jesus birth is in the book of Luke chapters one and two, starting with the story of Zachariah and Elisabeth conceiving John the Baptist. Zachariah was doing his service as a priest during the sacrifice of the season of Tabernacles and Yom Kippur, when the angel visited him. This time of celebration was usually in the autumn season.

The angel visited Mary during the Festival of Lights (Dedication of Lights) in the winter season in the month of December- January (John 8:12). She must have conceived and forty weeks later gave birth. The only place in the bible where there is mention of this season was when John mentioned it was the Feast of Dedication at Jerusalem (John 10:22).

As the angel finished speaking to Mary he told her that her cousin Elisabeth was pregnant also. Elisabeth was already pregnant for six months when Mary visited her. The scripture noted that on Mary's arrival the babies greeted each other in the spirit (Luke 1:36).

"I am come as a light into the world, that whosoever believeth on me should not abide in darkness."
John 12:46

The bible stated that it was during Passover season that Elisabeth gave birth. Mary had a few more months before her delivery during the Rosh Hashanah season, at the time of the annual sacrifice when the priest did the atonement. The Sages recorded the swaddling cloths were the priestly garments which were destroyed after they had killed the lamb of sacrifices at that time.

The women in those days were separated in the temple and the priest would place their bloody garments in baskets in their section. They would strip the garments into pieces of cloth for many things. They would be used for wicks for the lighting of the lamps in the temple. Some were used for wrapping wounds, maybe as in the case of the umbilical cord at the birth of a baby such as Jesus. The Hebrew word for swaddling clothes was *'Chatal'* - meaning a bandage.

"And Joseph also went up from Galilee, out of the city of Nazareth, into Judea, unto the city of David, which is called Bethlehem; (because he was of the house and lineage of David)
Luke 2-1-7

Chapter Twelve

Jesus Our High Priest

HIS BLESSINGS

The Lord wants to bless His people. Jesus didn't deserve to die, and even on the cross Jesus's last request to his father was to forgive them out of a heart of compassion. This meant that Jesus only wanted you and I to be blessed as He forgave our sins.

The Hebrew Sages noted that Jesus demonstrated His love as He ascended to heaven. The Jewish custom was that the people would bow their heads in honor to God in those days as the priestly blessing was being said over the assembly. Jesus, as He departed, began to say the priestly blessing and the disciples were in a reverent posture as He was lifted up into heaven.

The blessing of God is unto all who obey and do the command of the Lord. He told Moses to bless the people and as he did, the Lord promised to put His name on them (Numbers 6:22-27).

"I may cause those that love me to inherit substance; and I will fill their treasures."
Proverbs 8:21

The bible declared that God took His laws and wrote them on the tablet of your heart in order to make a covenant with you (Jeremiah 31:31-33). His desire is to bless you and gives you good health and prosperity. As you come to know Him, serve Him and surrender your will to His majesty, you receive the priestly blessings.

When we are rebellious and disobedient the opposite will occur. The scriptures say, the curses of your generations will be enforced upon you. God did put laws in place for blessing and curses in His word (Deuteronomy 28).

"For such that are blessed of him shall inherit the earth, and they that are cursed of him shall be cut off."
Psalm 37:22

HIS LOVE

The Lord's plan and desire from creation was for us to love and worship Him and do His work. He is looking for ones who develop a relationship that could capture God's heart. His intentions are to fellowship with us throughout our life and ministries. He wants man to be infused with a fresh relationship of daily communion with Him.

His commission is for all believers to demonstrate God's love and authority in power for healing and deliverance and to grow in alignment with God and to engage and desire to serve and work with him with great confidence in His promises. One scripture the Holy Ghost led me to was Isaiah 42:6-7.

I trusted the Lord to bring all His promises to pass. These gifts were used through the blood of Jesus to set at liberty those who the evil one tried to possess. He wants us to serve Him so that the devil will not have anything to gloat about.

"The Lord thy God in the midst of thee is mighty; he will save, he will rejoice over thee with joy; he will rest in his love, he will joy over you with singing."
Zephaniah 3:17

Jesus, in ancient times, had appointed seventy disciples to go and do the work in His name and the bible said they returned with joy and told Jesus that all the things He commissioned them to do they accomplished. The blind could see, the deaf heard, and the devils were subjected under them through His name. That did not move Jesus but, it was the following verse that stuck out. The scripture declared that Jesus said unto them, 'I beheld Satan as lightening fall from heaven.'

The revelation of the supernatural will increase as we continually do the work of Jesus. I suppose that the devil had no time to pack his back-pack as there was a quick discharge of electricity. I pray we would all come to that place that just as lightning, the enemies of our lives would fall, 'In Jesus name.'

"And Jesus came and spake unto them, saying, 'All power is given unto me in heaven and in earth. Go ye therefore, and teach tall nations, baptizing them in the name of the Father, and of the Son, and of the Holy Ghost: Teaching them to observe all things whatsoever I have commanded you: and lo, I am with you always, even unto the end of the world. Amen."
Matthew 28:18-20

His Liquid Love

March 2015, I dreamt: Early in the morning I was taken up into a heavenly experience. When I finally awoke, I could not remember what happened in my experience, it was something very odd but it felt great. I was upset and felt like the enemy stole my dream. I prayed to the Lord for a visitation and the following night my dream returned.

I was dancing and playing in a heavenly atmosphere with the Lord Jesus. I could see the beautiful colors of heaven; it felt as if I was floating in a silky rainbow-colored liquid, I was passing into it and through it with such happiness and unexplainable joy. I realized I could not go under or over this liquid. I was enjoying myself with the Lord, however, my mind couldn't comprehend what this really was. I heard the Lord say, 'EAT THE SCROLLS,' and I started eating them, and I continued eating them for a while. At that moment I had not a clue of what was taking place, but in my obedience I was in full compliance. Finally, it seemed like minutes had passed and I took courage to ask, 'Lord what is this?' and He answered, 'THIS IS GOD'S LIQUID LOVE.'

I woke up and contemplated what these words meant. I immediately, recorded in my notebook what I had just experienced. My mind pondered about this strange instruction as the spirit of the Lord lead me to the scripture in Revelation where the Lord told John to eat the scrolls. I was still deliberating the thought of God's Liquid Love for many days. I had never heard this terminology mentioned in any biblical scripts or by anyone at the time.

Early on Sunday morning the following week, the Lord woke me up and I felt a nudge to turn on the television to a Christian channel. To my amazement on the station there was a Pastor who was at that very moment saying his topic today would be on the LIQUID LOVE OF GOD.

"WOW! Jesus, you are so amazing!" was my response, "Thank you, Lord, this was unbelievable, I believe despite all my circumstances the Father God does love Me." This was all I kept uttering.

"Thy words were found, and I did eat them: and thy word was unto me the joy and rejoicing of mine heart: for I am called by thy name, O Lord God of Hosts."

Jeremiah 15:16

Chapter Thirteen

A Supernatural Surprise

"Jesus answered and said unto him, 'If a man loves me, he will keep my words: and my father will love him, and WE will come unto him, and make our abode with.'"
John 14:23

THE FATHER'S ENCOUNTER

July 27, 2015. It was 5 a.m. I named this, "A Supernatural Surprise" which has made a great impact on my walk as a believer.

I had a vision where, I saw fire fall from heaven. I was startled by the great explosion and I scrambled to wake up my honey, I asked him if he heard anything to which he replied that he heard a boom. I started crying for God to spare us and to have mercy over this nation and the world. Awake now, I found myself lying on the bed crying loudly, then suddenly, there came a thunderous and echoing voice from the Father God. I began to experience a prophetic utterance. As I heard Him say, "I am judging this nation."

I knew God was angry and that somehow judgement was upon the nation. The Father kept saying he was judging this nation, and he had thrown fire upon the White House and Washington DC. He said, there was a gathering in the white house and he was angry. He took me up, and I could see there were priest in long black gowns like Catholic's performing some ritual within a dark room with the heads of the state. I kept trying in my mind to plead for mercy for the people of America, but I could not control my mouth. I kept proclaiming judgement upon the nation. I could see fires all over the city of Washington DC and the buildings were crumbling. I knew we were all dead before it was over, yet I was a bit assured that I would be alive again, with the Lord's resurrection.

I heard myself saying, Rachem! Rachem! Rachem! This was part of my plea. My honey was right there but, he couldn't help me, I could not control myself from the body vibrations and shock waves in my spirit. I was conscious that my child had entered the room and knelt down by the bedside in reverence, of the presence of God that filled the room. I thought we all had been destroyed. Lord have mercy on the USA.

After my encounter, I found out the Hebrew word for *mercy* was RACHEM! My desire for learning Hebrew intensified. My life was never the same. I recognize the change immediately as, a divine acceleration took place in my spirit. My intercession intensified for Israel and the nations of the world.

I ventured in the bible for confirmation of such a visitation. I could not share with anyone what had happen for fear that they would judge me. I found in the book of Corinthians that the Apostle Paul acknowledged his fellowship with the three personalities of God. He reminded the believers that there are three levels of fellowship with God as 'Three in One.' He always gave honor to God the Father with love, the Lord Jesus Christ with grace, and the Holy Ghost with communion.

"For there are three that bear record in heaven, the Father, the Word (Jesus), and the Holy Ghost: and these are one."
1 John 5:7

PRAYER FOR AMERICA

One year in the month of February I heard the Holy spirit speak to me in my dreams. He instructed me to pray and declare these words: 'I push back the darkness in Jesus Name.'

As I repeated the instructions He said to declare, 'I Command the light of Christ to penetrate the darkness in Jesus Name.'

I did as he instructed me, and as I awoke I continued to exercise the prayer. I was not aware of the rioting that was exploding in Baltimore. The Lord was concerned about the riots that had broken out in the nation, and was presently in Baltimore City. During that week there were incidences escalating between the police and men of the city over a murder of an innocent man. The people had started a regiment of self-destruction to the neighborhoods and it was intensifying to a place that could have resulted in more killings. I began to pray for this situation and over the period of that very day, the situation came to a negotiation that resulted in a peaceful halt of the police and the people of the streets.

The Lord was even concerned about the welfare of the people. Thank you Lord for pushing back the darkness of the Spirit of Death in that region. The Lord loves all nations and peoples and He is concerned about their welfare.

I wondered what might have happened if those people had carried out the path of destruction. There would have been many lives lost, and my concern was how many would have been lost without Jesus Christ. Jesus's concern was for the lost souls, and His desire is that all nations including America would experience salvation.

"If my people, which are called by my name; shall humble themselves, and pray, and seek my face, and turn from their wicked ways; then will I hear from heaven, and will forgive their sin, and will heal their land."
(Your city and land are your life also)
2 Chronicles 7:14

Chapter Fourteen

The Master Craftsman

*"The Lord God formed man of the dust of the ground, and breathed into his
nostrils the breath of Life; and man became a living soul."*
Genesis 2:7

HIS CREATIVITY

The Ancient scholars found that there was a heavenly language in the
Ancient times. God is the Master craftsman and Creator of the Universe.

*"God created man in his own image, in the image of God created he him'
male and female created he them."*
Genesis 1:27

The scholars of Hebrew are still trying to figure out the workings of the
Lord. According to the scholars, from the fall of Adam everything
changed after he was cast out from the glory realm. They discovered that
the oldest language of Hebrew letters was in the time of Noah. They
noted that the era in which Noah and Abraham had lived, they were not

eloquent readers. God designed everything in pictorial formation to make their understanding simple and their memory permanent.

God told the story of His redemption plan in the formation made by the stars and the planets for the world. In the form of classical Hebrew script was the Ancient writing system. They were written in pictorial form as a representation of the Hebrew letters of their alphabet for easy reading and writing.

God works in the Supernatural realm was beyond man's comprehension. God in His miraculous splendor also designed an ability to function through creative miracles. In stories told in the bible the Lord performed supernatural miracles. He fed the multitude with seven loaves of bread and a few fish. He turned water into the best wine. He opened the eyes of the blind and made good limbs for the lame to walk. The bible says, He carried supernatural power as people reached out and touched Him they were made whole.

"For she said within herself, 'If I may but touch his garment, I shall be whole.' But Jesus turned him about, when he saw her, he said, 'Daughter, be of good comfort; thy faith hath made thee whole."
Matthew 9:20-22

King David inquired of the Lord for counsel. There was a war in the days of David and the Philistines were ambushing the Israelite camp. The Lord God gave David the strategy against his enemies on how to fight. The bible said that the Lord fought for His people as He had smitten all of their host (1 Chronicles 14).
Jesus throughout his ministry was a miracle working God. His gift of creative miracles was a norm in the supernatural realm beyond man's comprehension. He healed and delivered all those who were in need of a

miracle. He specialized in the impossible cases and He became famous as one who was an awesome provider.

The bible says that He fed four thousand men, besides women and children with seven loaves and a few fish supernaturally. He turned water into wine for the wedding and He walked on the water as a sign to illustrate He is the living water.

"Then he saith to the man, 'Stretch forth thine hand.'" And he stretched forth; and it was restored whole, like as the other."
Matthew 12:13

HIS CREATIVE MIRACLE

A prayer of Intercession occurred on March 19, 2015. I dreamt: The Lord showed me a person who had demonic attacks; there was a hole in a part of their body. I could see tiny white maggots festering inside. I held my mouth with fear and astonishment. Then I started pleading with the Lord – 'Is there anything Lord, you can do about it?' I pleaded with the Lord for a long while it seemed. As I grabbed unto his feet, Jesus just stood there staring at me without a word. I somehow began pleading for Him to do a "CREATIVE MIRACLE!" Lord, something "SUPERNATURAL!" I kept asking Him, 'Lord is there anything TOO DIFFICULT for you?' He never answered me, he stood there quietly. I woke up crying, I feared the worst, I kept crying for Jesus to 'help me,' all that day. Between the crying, I found myself praying and breaking the sickness, off of the individual. I plead, "THE BLOOD OF JESUS!" and commanded the creative miracle in Jesus Name. I had never heard anyone say those words before, but I trusted the Lord and he placed this language into my heart.

In my heart, I felt a lot of sadness; I felt like this person was going to lose to death. I prayed – 'I BREAK EVERY TIME-RELEASED

CURSE that would activate in their life as they grew older in JESUS NAME.'

Thanks to Jesus, the miracle of life had been performed and the person was healed and delivered.

A VALIDATION

It was about 10 a.m. in the morning when I dreamt that I was sitting around a foyer in a church building as I saw a pastor I had seen on television. When he arrived he came and sat at the same table where I was reading the word of God. We started a conversation and he seemed surprised to see me sitting all alone when there were other people standing around. I became very apologetic as I explained my reason for being there to him. I began to explain why I have to be still, for the Lord oftentimes revealed things in a Hebrew understanding to me.

He smiled and immediately began to pray and to prophecy over me, as he said the Lord would have many miracles performed in this ministry. He continued to say that he saw the setting of captives free and the loosing of those who were in bonds of wickedness.

I could see myself fall to the floor under the anointing as the Holy Ghost gripped my soul. It was a confirmation of a scripture the Holy Ghost had given me two days before (Isaiah 42:6). It seemed that I was groaning in the presence of God and it woke me up. I cried, 'I am available to you Lord!'

"I the Lord have called thee in righteousness, and will hold thine hand, and will keep thee, and give thee for a covenant of the people, for a light of the Gentiles; to open the blind eyes, to bring out the prisoners from the prison, and them that sit in darkness out of the prison house."
Isaiah 42:6-7

"The grace of the Lord Jesus Christ, and the love of God, and the communion of the Holy Ghost, be with you all. Amen."
2 Corinthians 13:14

Chapter Fifteen

His Truth Revisited

Jesus was the promised Messiah to the Jewish people. He was the fulfilment of the prophecies from the prophets of ancient times. He came out of the lineage of King David the patriarch of Israel. No other group of people can change His life story.

HIS LANGUAGE

Jesus spoke in a heavenly language, like his Father God. The Holy Ghost is the interpreter of the heavenly language and He speaks according to our nationality.

The Jewish historians proved that Jesus spoke Hebrew which was the language of the Jews or the Hebrews in the ancient times. Jesus spoke in his mother-tongue as all children of Israel did which was Hebrew which had been the language of their bible scriptures. Jesus would also have spoken Greek and Latin because of the cultures around at that particular time. It was mentioned on his cross. Jesus as God can speak through the Holy Spirit every language, even today.

"And Pilate wrote a title, and put it on the cross. And the writing was, Jesus of Nazareth The King of the Jews.' This title then read many of the Jews: for the place where Jesus was crucified was nigh the city: and it was written in Hebrew and Greek, and Latin."

John 19:19-20

The people who had encounters with the Holy Ghost had referred to this as 'other tongues.' It was noted that they were devoured men out of every nation under heaven, it was said that every man heard them speak in his own language. The people who heard them were amazed and marveled and they knew the disciple were all Galileans who only spoke Hebrew (Acts 2:3-7).

"And they were all filled with the Holy Ghost, and began to speak with other tongues, as the spirit gave them utterance." (the Heavenly Language)

Acts 2:4

King David in his last words acknowledges that Lord through a heavenly language spoke to him in the Hebrew Language (2 Samuel 23:2). The apostle Peter taught the people that the prophecy of old time came not by the will of man: but the holy men of God spoke as they were moved by the Holy Ghost (2 Peter 1:2).

HIS HEBREW LESSON

It was a Saturday around dawn, on October 9th, that I had just closed my eyes after praying. As Jesus appeared to me, it was a clear sunny day. He had a human frame and a wreath of thorns with a few dried leaves upon his head. I gazed in astonishment as he looked into my face with his penetrating eyes, and I heard him say: 'HEY DALET YOD ZAYIM.' I understood his words, as I repeat them to him in my heart in Hebrew.

His presence filled my atmosphere as He stood for a little while just gazing at me and then he disappeared.

"Lord thank you, for my lesson in Hebrew," I responded as I sat up and immediately wrote the words in my notebook. I was curious to understand the meaning of what he had said as he looked so intensely at me. I knew the letters but I began to research the meaning of those words. The Hebrew alphabet was the guideline to find their numeric value.

My calculations I hope will inspire someone to learn a little Hebrew. The Hebrew language is a unique and holy language. It has a modern and ancient writing that is multi-faceted. I prefer the ancient writings because of the pictorial system. It includes a sound, a numerical value and a sacred meaning. It is easier to understand the hidden truth in each demonstration as the basic letters of the alphabet are amazing. This is another way you can see the humor in the Lord.

AN ILLUSTRATION

HEY = 5   DALET = 4   YOD = 10   ZAYIM = 7   TOTAL = 26

'Hey' means Behold as something revealed. It is a picture of a man with his arms raised and means: the presence of God within the human heart. Its numeric value is 5 meaning the number of grace.

"And God said, 'Let there be light': and there was light. And God saw the light, that it was good: and God divided the light from the darkness." (Hey!)
Genesis 1:3-4

'Dalet' represents the door in Hebrew or a pathway. Its pictorial view symbolizes a bent over man, meaning "to draw out" or impoverished. Its numeric value is 4.

"Behold, I stand at the door and Knock, if any man hears my voice, and open the door, I will come in to him, and will sup with him, and he with me."
Revelation3:20 (Dalet)

'Yod' represents a hand, also has been a mark of humility or meekness. It pictorial view is tiny curve, it is considered the smallest letter in the alpha-bet. Its numeric value is 10, marking completion or order and it is also a mystery number.

"The Lord did not set his love upon you, nor choose you, because ye were more in number than any people; for ye were the fewest of all people that are upon the earth."
Deuteronomy 7:7 (Yod)

In Hebrew commentary, it is noted that the letter 'YOD' is a representation of a little nation called Israel. The Hebrew scholars said, the story is told, that God delights in using the small, the weak, and the insignificant to demonstrate His glory and power.

'Zayim' represents a nail or a sword that was used to defend or fasten things. The pictorial view of a sword or nail was a type of weapon. Its numeric value is 7, meaning the number of completion, wholeness, blessing and rest. The sword can also represent our Protector, as Jesus is 'The Lion of the Tribe of Judah' or a depiction of Jesus as the Shepherd who feeds His sheep.

"For the word of God is quick and powerful, and sharper than any two-edged sword, piercing even to the dividing asunder of soul and spirit, and of the joints and marrow, and is a discerner of the thoughts and intents of the heart."

Hebrew 4:12 (Zayim)

The sum of the numeric value of each word is 26. The number 26 is the numeric value of the name of the Lord God (Yahweh – meaning Merciful God)

The total accolade for such a depiction of the Hebrew letters and numbers presented the statement of "Behold, 'Yeshua'- Jesus nailed to a cross as the pathway to salvation and Deliverance."

PEACE FOR JERUSALEM

"Pray for the Peace of Jerusalem: They shall prosper that love thee. Peace be within thy walls, and prosperity within thy palaces."
Psalm 122:6-7

It was on March 26, 2015 when I was singing this Hebrew song – Kadosh, Kadosh, El Shaddai, Adonai, this means "Holy, Holy, Lord God Almighty." I had begun listening to Hebrew music for some time, so I understood what I was saying. In my dream there were explosions and buildings were being blown up.

All around me, as far as my eyes could see there were huge stones and debris falling from buildings. It seemed as though the scenery was in Israel. I could see the city was not that huge and there were many tall buildings to provide living spaces. I felt like I was praying for the people and the peace of the land. I could hear an echoing voice from the heavens saying, 'DRINK MY BLOOD AND YOU WILL LIVE!' The people who drank the blood, as it was flowing down from the heavens, those people were able to get cover from the danger and they survived. There were angels of the Lord who were swiftly ushering them to safety and we went into an underground channel. There was much devastation and I prayed for the people of Israel that their eyes would be open to their Messiah.

"I have chosen Jerusalem, that my name might be there."
2 Chronicles 6:6

The Lord loves the people of Israel. He chose them over all the nations. Jerusalem has significance to the Lord Jesus Christ, it is claimed as God's land in the bible. The title deed was found in the transaction between Abraham and Ephron. (Genesis 23: 13-16) The historic evidence of this city is of the past, the present and the future of the world. Jesus rode a donkey into the city Jerusalem to declare himself as the Messiah to the nation and the scriptures declares He will in the future return to that land.

The Lord said, He would bless the people who pray for Jerusalem's peace and safety. For believers this is a command we should obey. I was impressed as I read the book of Joel 3:17-18.

"So, shall ye know that I am the Lord your God dwelling in Zion, my holy mountain: then shall Jerusalem be holy, and there shall no stranger pass through her any more. And it shall come to pass in that day, that the mountains shall drop down new wine, and the hills shall flow with milk, and all the rivers of Judah shall flow with waters, and a fountain shall come forth of the house of the Lord, and shall water the valley of Shittim."
(The restoration of Israel)
Joel 3:17-18

Chapter Sixteen

His Attributes

HIS BAPTISM OF FIRE

The Holy Ghost's fire is the gift that empowers you to achieve the work of God. Everyone can receive the baptism of the Holy Ghost by faith in Jesus Christ. This gift is part of the evidence of your new birth of salvation and redemption. The bible declares that Jesus had to die in order for us to receive his Ghost, or the Holy Ghost.

On July 2, 2015 I was relaxing in bed, worshipping in my heart and suddenly, the Lord visited me and I experienced the baptism of His Holy Ghost fire. I had an experience of the fire of God with evidence of speaking in tongues, but this was different. The weight of His power I could not resist. As I laid there shaking, the Lord said, "I have marked you for my work." In that moment, I was empowered with a boldness to do the work of God. I saw a drastic change and even my family recognized that something was different in my desire for more of the Lord and His word.

"And suddenly there came a sound from heaven as a rushing mighty wind, and filled all the house where they were sitting. And there appeared unto them cloven tongues like as of fire, and it sat upon each of them. And they were filled with the Holy Ghost, and began to speak with other tongues, as the Spirit gave them utterance."
Acts 2: 2-4

The Lord imprinted a new heart in me and my walk and conversations with the Lord are a great pleasure each day. I am more understanding of my unworthy condition, yet His grace and mercy covers me. Like the psalmist declared,

"Thou hast clothed me with skin and flesh, and has fenced me with bones and sinews. Thou hast granted me life and favor, and Thy visitation hath preserved my spirit."
Job 10:11-12

"I will praise Thee, for I am fearfully and wonderfully made: and my soul knoweth right well. My substance was not hid from Thee. Thine eyes did see my substance, yet being unperfect; and Thy book all my members were written, which in continuance were fashioned when as yet there was none of them. How precious also are Thy thoughts unto me. O GOD! How great is the sum of them?"
Psalms 138:14-18

His Anointing Oil

A lesson I learned was that Jesus secures, as there is protection in the anointing of the head. The Psalmist David said, *"He anointed my head with Oil"* (Psalm 23:5). The oil was a symbol of God at work in a person's life. The prophet anointed David the shepherd to become king in Saul's place (1 Samuel 16:13). The bible declares that the Lord told Moses to anoint Aaron and his sons for the priestly work in the Tabernacle. The scriptures say that the righteous should always wear white and clean garments, and always let their head lack no oil (Ecclesiastes 9:8).

One Tuesday morning at 8 a.m. my son woke me up as he was about to leave the house. He was leaving for the studio with some friends. I decided to get in the shower and freshen up. As I got in I heard the Lord whisper softly, 'You didn't anoint your boy's head today.' He literally called his name. I responded with my reason as I explained to the Lord that my son usually does this by himself. This was my way of excusing myself, however, I asked the Lord to keep him safe through his journey.

It was not even five minutes after the Lord had spoken that, I received a phone call and there was my son on the other end. The news of the incident was astounding as he explained that, they were driving and one of the car wheels had broken off and flew onto the highway ahead of them. He continued to explain the scary experience; however, they were okay. He concluded with their response of screams for Jesus to help, during the ordeal.

With a grateful heart, I thank the Lord for watching over the children. He showed love and compassion as he made my heart began to pray for their safety. At that very moment they need his protection from danger. Later, I inquired and found out that my son had not anointed himself because he was rushing that morning.

After he arrived home, he eventually detailed the incident and it was incredible what the Lords had done. There were no other cars in the vicinity of incident on the road. Thanks to the Lord, as the other parents were praying too. 'Thank you for your guarding Angels' who protect our children always, with a grateful heart.'

"Hast thou not known? Hast thou not heard, that the everlasting God, the Lord, the Creator of the ends of the earth, fainteth not, neither is weary? There is no searching of his understanding. He giveth power to the faint; and to them that have no might he increaseth strength."
Isaiah 40:28-29

Chapter Seventeen

His Empowerment Skills

"The Lord of Hosts is wonderful in counsel, and excellent in working."
Isaiah 28:29

HIS COUNSEL

His counsel is divine, it can be referred to His heavenly hosts. Yet it can be said that God rules and maintains the universe. His Holy Spirit will guide you into truth and revelations like only God can do.

The apostle Paul shared everything that the Lord had revealed to him about the whole counsel of God. God had extended his plan of salvation to all, and his will is for all to come to know the Truth. He is a God of revelation, wisdom and understanding; everything comes from him (Proverbs 1:7). The counsel of God is vital as a believer for it is the access to the spiritual realm of revelation and knowledge from the Lord Jesus. When Jesus is invited into your everyday walk, His Holy Spirit becomes involve in strengthening you to achieve His will in your life.

In ancient times the Kings and Prophet sought the Lord's counsel for many decisions they had to make pertaining to situations of wars and moving to other places. They even consulted with the Lord for the anointing of kings and apostles. The bible declared that King David inquired of the Lord (2 Samuel 2:1).

God's word becomes illuminated in your heart as you seek after His righteous counsel. The bible declared that many of the prophets had an intimate relationship with the Lord. He walked and talked with them through His word and by faith. This encourages the letting go of every distraction that can hinder your friendship with Jesus. It also required having a lifestyle that aligns and reflects the person of Jesus Christ.

"In that same hour Jesus rejoiced in spirit, and said, I thank thee, O Father, Lord of heaven and earth, that thou hast hid these things from the wise and prudent, and hast revealed them unto babes: even so, Father; for so it seemed good in thy sight."
Luke 10:21

HIS PROMISE

God from the foundation of the world had a great plan for human lives. This was a promise that we should share eternal life with Jesus Christ (1 John 5:11). The bible declares that God's promise and plan is for you to live in happiness and peace, health and prosperity (Jeremiah 29:11).

As you acknowledge his Lordship you will receive access by the blood of Jesus and by faith. Jesus is the same yesterday, today and forever. There will be a marriage in the coming of our Lord if you will hold fast to his promises.

"The God of our Lord Jesus, the Father of Glory, may give unto you the spirit of wisdom and revelation in the knowledge of Him: The eyes of you understanding being enlightened; that ye may know what is the hope of his calling, and what the riches of his glory of his inheritance in the saints."
Ephesians 1:17-18

As you aspire to become intimate with the Lord, you will gradually develop a surrendered reverence. The word of God will come alive in greater dimensions. The glory of the Lord shall descend in a greater measure in your life as you allow the Holy Spirit to do His work in you. The promise of rivers flowing out of your belly is rivers of healing, wisdom, discernment, revelations and all the gifts of the spirit.

"He that believeth on me, as the scripture hath said, 'Out of his belly shall flow rivers of living water.'" (The Holy Spirit)
John 7:38

The apostle Paul gave us great encouragement to walk in faith with the Lord Jesus Christ. You know that all things work together for good to them that love God, to them who are the called according to his purpose (Romans 8:28).

HE IS LORD!

One more thing I found fascinating about Jesus is that he has no fear. He is the most confident person I have ever known. He is always rooting for you to succeed.

Many people start out excited to love and follow Jesus. Then life events and circumstances which occur influence people to turn away and abort their destiny. You must be reminded what a loving and

97

compassionate God he is, as you recall and remember the mercy you have received throughout your days.

"Come unto me, all ye that labour and are heavy laden, and I will give you rest."
Matthew 11:28

As a loving Father He leads us in the way of righteousness. The prophet Nehemiah's confession touched the heart of the Lord. You should always be appreciative of all the small and great things the Lord has done for you.

Nehemiah declared,

"Yet thou in thy manifold mercies forsook them not in the wilderness: The pillar of the cloud departed not from them by day, to lead them in the way, neither the pillar of fire by night, to show them light and the way wherein they should go."
Nehemiah 9:19

It is very overwhelming when I think of how Jesus rescued me from sin and condemnation. It took much determination to have faith and take time to pray and worship the Lord. The Lord has so much to teach you, it will blow your mind. The revelation and knowledge acquired will make your academic achievements seem like little.

This book is comprised of lessons I have learned as I took the time to get to know Jesus as a friend and Savior. He is the Lord of all lords, God of all gods, and King of all kings.

"Let your light so shine before men, that they may see your good works, and glorify your Father which is in heaven."

(Let your language of Love reflect the Father's Love for us.)
Matthew 5:16

HOW TO EXPERIENCE JESUS

HIS INVITATION

Jesus Christ is standing and awaiting your response. He extends an invitation to you, no matter what the circumstances are in your life.

It is time for your visitation. I pray that your desire for personal friendship with Jesus Christ is activated. He loves and cares for you like no one can, and He desires to be closer to you and to bless you. I know He longs to awaken you to his supernatural nature. He will speak with you and dwell in you for all eternity.

My challenge to you is to take a step of faith in the direction of prayer and reading the word of God. As you cultivate a worship atmosphere for the presence of the Lord, let your mindset be with great expectation for the change. Jesus will equip you with power to overcome that sly old devil in your pathways.

"Ho everyone that thirst, come ye to the waters, and he that had no money; come ye buy and eat."
Isaiah 55:1

It is vital that we repent and cleanse our life of all the hinderance of sins so that we can have an experience with the Spirit of the Lord. You can pray and ask the Lord for His help for there is a transformation that happens in the moment you call upon Jesus. It is a process of surrendering, and little by little the new revelation of Jesus will manifest.

I pray today that the Lord will come and rescue you wherever you are spiritually and place you on the path to a spiritual encounter with him.

A PRAYER FOR REPENTANCE:

Lord Jesus I turn back to your original plans and instructions for my life. Please forgive me of all my sins and transgressions. I acknowledge my iniquities and ask for cleansing from all generational curses. Thank you for dying on the cross for my sins. Deliver me with your precious blood. Restore the joy of my salvation. Draw me near and teach me insights that come from you. Strengthen me to put my hope in you. Bless me with your life and peace. In Jesus name I pray. Amen.

Lord, I pray that the same deliverance I received, that you would grant my reader to be free to hear the voice of the Lord. Pour out your love into their hearts by your Holy Spirit (Romans 5:5).

"Hope maketh not ashamed; because the Love of God is shed abroad in our hearts by the Holy Ghost which is given unto us. For when we were yet without strength, in due time Christ died for the ungodly."
Roman 5:5-6

About the Author

Wynette A. Tyrrell is a child of God who's been serving the Lord for many years and the gift of the Holy Spirit is evident in her service to God as His love radiates through her life and ministry. From an early age, she had always experienced dreams and visions of the Lord. The appearance of Jesus came to her in several ways – in dreams, visions and by revelation of the word of God.

Wynette's passion is to see people transformed by the presence and power of God. She loves to see people come into an intimate relationship with Him. As a teacher of the gospel, her work transcends all ages with a unique ability that causes her audience to experience the person of Jesus Christ and our heavenly Father. Her experiences are marked with supernatural activities of miracles, healings, and deliverance.

Wynette is a loving and devoted wife. Together with her husband they parent two amazing children. In her time of fun, she and her entire family loves racing cars. She also enjoys reading and has a special love for babies. As a people's person, she "loves to love."